PAT
Practice Papers

UniAdmissions

Published by *RAR Medical Services Limited*
www.uniadmissions.co.uk
info@uniadmissions.co.uk
Tel: 0208 068 0438

PAT Practice Papers

5 Full Papers & Solutions

Samuel Putra
Dr Rohan Agarwal

UniAdmissions

About the Authors

Samuel is currently a third-year DPhil candidate in Engineering Science at Trinity College, University of Oxford. He obtained his MEng degree from Oxford with First-Class Honours, graduating in the top 4% of his class. Since his undergraduate years, Samuel has assisted many A  level students with their university admissions, providing tuition for entrance exam preparation and guidance for interviews.

During his postgraduate study, Samuel holds a teaching role as Graduate Teaching Assistant at Oxford, providing tutorials for undergraduates in Chemical Engineering Modules. His research is focused on Sustainable Wastewater Treatment and Energy Recovery which has secured several awards including Best Poster in Water Category at Concawe Symposium 2017. In his spare time, Samuel enjoys going to the gym and playing football.

Rohan is the **Director of Operations** at *UniAdmissions* and is responsible for its technical and commercial arms. He graduated from Gonville and Caius College, Cambridge and is a fully qualified doctor. Over the last five years, he has tutored hundreds of successful Oxbridge and Medical applicants. He has also authored fifty books on admissions tests and interviews.

Rohan has taught physiology to undergraduates and interviewed medical school applicants for Cambridge. He has published research on bone physiology and writes education articles for the Independent and Times. In his spare time, Rohan enjoys playing the piano and table tennis.

Introduction

The Basics

The Physics Aptitude Test (PAT) is the 100 mark, 2-hour, written aptitude exam taken by students applying for physics, materials science and engineering courses at the University of Oxford.

It is a highly time pressured exam that forces you to apply your physics knowledge in ways you have never thought about before. In this respect simply remembering solutions taught in class or from past papers is not enough.

However, fear not, despite what people say, you can actually prepare for the PAT! With a little practice you can train your brain to manipulate and apply learnt methodologies to novel problems with ease. The best way to do this is through exposure to as many past/specimen papers as you can.

Preparing for the PAT

Past PAT papers are freely available online at - **www.uniadmissions.co.uk/every-past-papers-answer-sheets/** and serve as excellent practice. You're strongly advised to use these in combination with the *PAT Past Worked Solutions* Book so that you can

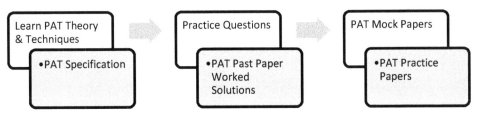

improve your weaknesses. Finally, once you've exhausted past papers, move onto the mock papers in this book.

Already seen them all?

So, you've run out of past papers? Well that is where this book comes in. This book contains five unique mock papers; each compiled by Oxford physics tutors at *UniAdmissions* and available nowhere else.

Having successfully gained a place on their course of choice, our tutors are intimately familiar with the PAT and its associated admission procedures. So, the novel questions presented to you here are of the correct style and difficulty to continue your revision and stretch you to meet the demands of the PAT.

General Advice

Start Early

It is much easier to prepare if you practice little and often. Start your preparation well in advance; ideally 10 weeks but at the latest within a month. This way you will have plenty of time to complete as many papers as you wish to feel comfortable and won't have to panic and cram just before the test, which is a much less effective and more stressful way to learn. In general, an early start will give you the opportunity to identify the complex issues and work at your own pace.

Prioritise

Some questions can be long and complex and, given the intense time pressure, you need to know your limits. It is essential that you don't get stuck with very difficult questions. If a question looks particularly long or complex, mark it for review and move on. You don't want to be caught 5 questions short at the end just because you took more than 3 minutes in answering a challenging multi-step question. If a question is taking too long, choose a sensible answer and move on. With practice and discipline, you can get very good at this and learn to maximise your efficiency.

Positive Marking

There are no penalties for incorrect answers; you will marks for each right answer and will not get any for each wrong or unanswered one. This provides you with the luxury that, on the multiple-choice questions, you can always guess should you absolutely be not able to figure out the right answer for a question or run behind time. Since each question provides you with 5 possible answers, you have a 20% chance of guessing correctly. Therefore, if you aren't sure (and are running short of time), then make an educated guess and move on. Before 'guessing' you should try to eliminate a couple of answers to increase your chances of getting the question correct. For example, if you manage to eliminate 2 options your chances of getting the question right increase from 20% to 33%!

Avoid losing easy marks on other questions because of poor exam technique. Similarly, if you have failed to finish the exam, take the last 10 seconds to guess the remaining questions to at least give yourself a chance of getting them right.

Practice

This is the best way of familiarising yourself with the style of questions and the timing. You are unlikely to be familiar with the style of questions in all sections when you first encounter them. Therefore, you want to be comfortable with this before you sit the test.

Practising questions will put you at ease and make you more comfortable with the exam. The more comfortable you are, the less you will panic on the test day and the more likely you are to score highly. Initially, work through the questions at your own pace, and spend time carefully reading the questions and looking at any additional data. When it becomes closer to the test, **make sure you practice the questions under exam conditions**.

Past Papers

Official past papers and answers from 2006 onwards are freely available online on our website at –

www.uniadmissions.co.uk/every-past-papers-answer-sheets/

You will undoubtedly get stuck when doing some past paper questions – they are designed to be tricky and the answer schemes don't offer any explanations. Thus, **you're highly advised to acquire a copy of PAT Past Paper Worked Solutions**.

Repeat Questions

When checking through answers, pay particular attention to questions you have got wrong. If there is a worked answer, look through that carefully until you feel confident that you understand the reasoning, and then repeat the question without help to check that you can do it. If only the answer is given, have another look at the question and try to work out why that answer is correct. This is the best way to learn from your mistakes, and means you are less likely to make similar mistakes when it comes to the test. The same applies for questions you were unsure of and made an educated guess, even if you got it right. When working through this book, **make sure you highlight any questions you are unsure of**, so that you know to spend more time looking over them once marked.

A word on timing...

"If you had all day to do your exam, you would get 100%. But you don't."

Whilst this isn't completely true, it illustrates a very important point. Once you've practiced and know how to answer the questions, the clock is your biggest enemy. This seemingly obvious statement has one very important consequence. **The way to improve your score is to improve your speed.** There is no magic bullet. But there are a great number of techniques that, with practice, will give you significant time gains, allowing you to answer more questions and score more marks.

Timing is tight throughout – **mastering timing is the first key to success**. Some candidates choose to work as quickly as possible to save up time at the end to check back, but this is generally not the best way to do it. Often questions can have a lot of information in them – each time you start answering a question it takes time to get familiar with the instructions and information. By splitting the question into two sessions (the first run-through and the return-to-check) you double the amount of time you spend on familiarising yourself with the data, as you have to do it twice instead of only once. This costs valuable time. In addition, candidates who do check back may spend 2–3 minutes doing so and yet not make any actual changes. Whilst this can be reassuring, it is a false reassurance as it is unlikely to have a significant effect on your actual score. Therefore, it is usually best to pace yourself very steadily, aiming to spend the same amount of time on each question and finish the final question in a section just as time runs out. This reduces the time spent on re-familiarising with questions and maximises the time spent on the first attempt, gaining more marks.

It is essential that you don't get stuck with the hardest questions – no doubt there will be some. In the time spent answering only one of these you may miss out on answering three easier questions. If a question is taking too long, choose a sensible answer and move on. Never see this as giving up or failing in any way, rather it is the smart way to approach a test with a tight time limit. With practice and discipline, you can get very good at this and learn to maximise your efficiency. It is not about being a hero and aiming for full marks – this is almost impossible and very much unnecessary. It is about maximising your efficiency and gaining the highest possible number of marks within the time you have.

Use the Options:

Some questions may try to overload you with information. When presented with large tables and data, it's essential you look at the answer options so you can focus your mind. This can allow you to reach the correct answer a lot more quickly. Consider the example below:

The table below shows the results of a study investigating antibiotic resistance in staphylococcus populations. A single staphylococcus bacterium is chosen at random from a similar population. Resistance to any one antibiotic is independent of resistance to others.

Antibiotic	Number of Bacteria tested	Number of Resistant Bacteria
Benzyl-penicillin	10^{11}	98
Chloramphenicol	10^9	1200
Metronidazole	10^8	256
Erythromycin	10^5	2

Calculate the probability that the bacterium selected will be resistant to all four drugs.

A. 1 in 10^6 C. 1 in 10^{20} E. 1 in 10^{30}
B. 1 in 10^{12} D. 1 in 10^{25}

Looking at the options first makes it obvious that there is **no need to calculate exact values** - only in powers of 10. This makes your life a lot easier. If you hadn't noticed this, you might have spent well over 90 seconds trying to calculate the exact value when it wasn't even being asked for.

In other cases, you may actually be able to use the options to arrive at the solution quicker than if you had tried to solve the question as you normally would. Consider the example below:

A region is defined by the two inequalities: $x - y^2 > 1 \land xy > 1$. Which of the following points is in the defined region?

A. (10,3)   D. (-10,2)
B. (10,2)   E. (-10,-3)
C. (-10,3)

Whilst it's possible to solve this question both algebraically or graphically by manipulating the identities, by far **the quickest way is to actually use the options**. Note that options C and D violate the second inequality, narrowing down the answer to either A, B or E. For A: $10 - 3^2 = 1$ and thus this point is on the boundary of the defined region and not actually in the region. For E: $-10 - (-3)^2 = -19$ and thus this point violates the first inequality. Therefore the answer is B (as $10 - 4 = 6 > 1$).

In general, it pays dividends to look at the options briefly and see if they can help you arrive at the question more quickly. Get into this habit early – it may feel unnatural at first but it's guaranteed to save you **time in the long run.**

Manage your Time:

It is highly likely that you will be juggling your revision alongside your normal school studies. Whilst it is tempting to put your A-levels on the back burner, falling behind in your school subjects is not a good idea – don't forget that to meet the conditions of your offer should you get one you will need at least one A*. So, time management is key!

Make sure you set aside a dedicated **90 minutes** (and much more closer to the exam) to commit to your revision each day. The key here is not to sacrifice too many of your extracurricular activities (everybody needs some down time) but instead to be efficient. Take a look at our list of top tips for increasing revision efficiency below:

1. Create a comfortable workstation: declutter and stay tidy.
2. Treat yourself to some nice stationery.
3. See if music works for you – if not, find somewhere peaceful and quiet to work.
4. Turn off your mobile or at least put it into silent mode and silence social media alerts.
5. Keep the TV off and out of sight.
6. Stay organised with to do lists and revision timetables – more importantly, stick to them!
7. Keep to your set study times and don't bite off more than you can chew.
8. Study while you're commuting.
9. Adopt a positive mental attitude.
10. Get into a routine.
11. Consider forming a study group to focus on the harder exam concepts.
12. Plan rest and reward days into your timetable – these are excellent incentives for you to stay on track with your study plans!

Keep Fit & Eat Well:

'A car won't work if you fill it with the wrong fuel' - your body is exactly the same. You cannot hope to perform unless you remain fit and well. The best way to do this is to not underestimate the importance of healthy eating. Beige, starchy foods will make you sluggish; instead start the day with a hearty breakfast like porridge. Aim for the recommended 'five a day' intake of fruit/veg and stock up on the oily fish or blueberries – the so called "super foods".

When hitting the books, it's essential to keep your brain hydrated. If you get dehydrated you'll find yourself lethargic and possibly developing a headache, neither of which will do any favours for your revision. Invest in a good water bottle so that you know the total volume of water you've drunk and keep sipping throughout the day. Don't forget that the amount of water you should be aiming to drink varies depending on your mass, so calculate your own personal recommended intake as follows: 30 ml per kg per day.

It is well known that exercise boosts your wellbeing and instils a sense of discipline, both of which will reflect well in your revision. It is well worth devoting half an hour a day to some exercise, get your heart rate up, break a sweat, and get those endorphins flowing.

Sleep

It's no secret that when revising you need to keep well rested. Don't be tempted to stay up late revising as sleep actually plays an important part in consolidating long term memory. Instead aim for a minimum of 7 hours good sleep each night, in a dark room without any glow from electronic appliances. Install flux (https://justgetflux.com) on your laptop to prevent your computer from disrupting your circadian rhythm. Aim to go to bed the same time each night and no hitting snooze on the alarm clock in the morning!

Revision Timetable

Still struggling to get organised? Then try filling in the example revision timetable below (remember to factor in enough time for short breaks) and stick to it! Remember to schedule in several breaks throughout the day and actually use them to do something you enjoy e.g. TV, reading, YouTube etc.

	8AM	10AM	12PM	2PM	4PM	6PM	8PM
MONDAY							
TUESDAY							
WEDNESDAY							
THURSDAY							
FRIDAY							
SATURDAY							
SUNDAY							

Top tip! Ensure that you take a watch that can show you the time in seconds into the exam. This will allow you have a much more accurate idea of the time you're spending on a question.

Getting the most out of Mock Papers

Mock exams can prove invaluable if tackled correctly. Not only do they encourage you to start revision earlier, they also allow you to **practice and perfect your revision technique**. They are often the best way of improving your knowledge base or reinforcing what you have learnt. Probably the best reason for attempting mock papers is to familiarise yourself with the exam conditions of the PAT as they are particularly tough.

Start revision earlier

Thirty five percent of students agree that they procrastinate to a degree that is detrimental to their exam performance. This is partly explained by the fact that they often seem a long way in the future. In the scientific literature this is well recognised – Dr. Piers Steel, an expert on the field of motivation states that *'the further away an event is, the less impact it has on your decisions'*.

Mock exams are therefore a way of giving you a target to work towards and motivate you in the run up to the real thing – every time you do one treat it as the real deal! If you do well then it's a reassuring sign; if you do poorly then it will motivate you to work harder (and earlier!).

Practice and perfect revision techniques

In case you haven't realised already, revision is a skill all to itself and can take some time to learn. For example, the most common revision techniques including **highlighting and/or re-reading are quite ineffective** ways of committing things to memory. Unless you are thinking critically about something you are much less likely to remember it or indeed understand it.

Mock exams therefore allow you to test your revision strategies as you go along. Try spacing out your revision sessions so you have time to forget what you have learnt in-between. This may sound counterintuitive but the second time you remember it for longer. Try teaching another student what you have learnt – this forces you to structure the information in a logical way that may aid memory. Always try to question what you have learnt and appraise its validity. Not only does this aid memory but it is also a useful skill for Oxbridge interviews and beyond.

Improve your knowledge
The act of applying what you have learnt reinforces that piece of knowledge. A question may ask you to think about a relatively basic concept in a novel way (not cited in textbooks), and so deepen your understanding. Exams rarely test word for word what is in the syllabus, so when running through mock papers try to understand how the basic facts are applied and tested in the exam. As you go through the mocks or past papers take note of your performance and see if you consistently under-perform in specific areas, thus highlighting areas for future study.

Get familiar with exam conditions
Pressure can cause all sorts of trouble for even the most brilliant students. The PAT is a particularly time pressured exam with high stakes – your future (without exaggerating) does depend on your result to a great extent. The real key to the PAT is overcoming this pressure and remaining calm to allow you to think efficiently.

Mock exams are therefore an excellent opportunity to devise and perfect your own exam techniques to beat the pressure and meet the demands of the exam. **Don't treat mock exams like practice questions – it's imperative you do them under time conditions.**

Remember! It's better that you make all the mistakes you possibly can now in mock papers and then learn from them so as not to repeat them in the real exam.

Before using this Book

Do the ground work

- Read in detail: the background, methods, and aims of the PAT as well logistical considerations such as how to take the PAT in practice.
    - It is generally a good idea to start recapping all your GCSE and AS maths.
- Get comfortable rapidly converting between percentages, decimals, and fractions.
- These are all things which are easiest to do alongside your revision for exams before the summer break. You will not only gain a head start on your PAT revision, but this will also compliment your year 12 studies well.
- Discuss topical physics problems with others - propose theories and be ready to defend your argument. This will rapidly build your scientific understanding but also prepare you well for an Oxbridge interview.
- Read through the PAT syllabus before you start tackling whole papers. This is absolutely essential. It contains several stated formulae, constants, and facts that you are expected to apply - or may just be an answer in their own right. Familiarising yourself with the syllabus is also a quick way of teaching yourself the additional information other exam boards may learn which you do not.

Ease in gently

With the groundwork laid, there's still no point in adopting exam conditions straight away. Instead invest in a beginner's guide to the PAT, which will not only describe in detail the background and theory of the exam but take you through what is expected section by section.

When you are ready to move on to past papers, take your time and puzzle your way through all the questions. Really try to understand solutions. A past paper question won't be repeated in your real exam, so don't rote learn methods or facts. Instead, focus on applying prior knowledge to formulate your own approach.

If you're really struggling and have to take a sneak peek at the answers, then practice thinking of alternative solutions. It is unlikely that your answer will be more elegant or succinct than the model answer, but it is still a good task for encouraging creativity with your thinking. Get used to thinking outside the box!

Accelerate and Intensify

Start adopting exam conditions after you've done two past papers. Don't forget that **it's the time pressure that makes the PAT hard** – if you had as long as you wanted to sit the exam you would probably get 100%. If you're struggling to find comprehensive answers to past papers then PAT *Past Papers Worked Solutions* contains detailed explained answers to every PAT past paper question.

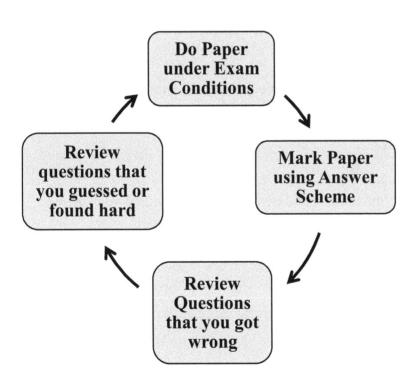

Doing every past paper at least twice is a good target for your revision. In any case, choose a paper and proceed with strict exam conditions. Take a short break and then mark your answers before reviewing your progress. For revision purposes, as you go along, keep track of those questions that you guess – these are equally as important to review as those you get wrong.

Once you've exhausted all the past papers, move on to tackling the unique mock papers in this book. In general, you should aim to complete one to two mock papers every night in the ten days preceding your exam.

How to use this Book

If you have done everything this book has described so far then you should be well equipped to meet the demands of the PAT, and therefore **the mock papers in the rest of this book should ONLY be completed under exam conditions**.

This means:

- Absolute silence – no TV or music.
- Absolute focus – no distractions such as eating your dinner.
- Strict time constraints – no pausing halfway through.
- No checking the answers as you go.
- Complete the entire paper before marking and then mark harshly.

In practice this means setting aside two hours in an evening to find a quiet spot without interruptions and tackle the paper. Completing one mock paper every evening in the week running up to the exam would be an ideal target.

- Tackle the paper as you would in the exam.
- Return to mark your answers but mark harshly if there's any ambiguity.
- Highlight any areas of concern.
- If warranted read up on the areas you felt you underperformed to reinforce your knowledge.
- If you inadvertently learnt anything new by muddling through a question, go and tell somebody about it to reinforce what you've discovered.

Finally, relax... the PAT is an exhausting exam, concentrating so hard continually for two hours will take its toll. So, being able to relax and switch off is essential to keep yourself sharp for exam day! Make sure you reward yourself after you finish marking your exam.

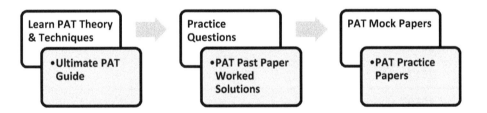

Scoring Tables

Use these to keep a record of your scores from past papers and these mock papers – you can then easily see which paper you should attempt next (always the one with the lowest score).

Past Paper	1st Attempt	2nd Attempt	3rd Attempt
2006	10 /22		
2007	8 /22		
2008	14/21		
2009	12.7/21		
2010			
2011			
2012			
2013			
2014			
2015			
2016			
2017			
2018			
2019			

Paper	1st Attempt	2nd Attempt	3rd Attempt
A			
B			
C			
D			
E			

Mock Paper A

Question 1:

Differentiate $y = 5x^2 \sin 2x$ with respect to x.

A. $10x(x \cos 2x - \sin 2x)$

B. $10x(x \cos 2x + \sin 2x)$

C. $10x(x^2 \cos 2x + \sin 2x)$

D. $5x(x \cos 2x + \sin 2x)$

E. $10x(x \sin 2x + \cos 2x)$

Question 2:

If $x = 1$ is a root of the equation $2x^3 + x^2 - 5x = -2$, find the other two roots.

A. $x = 1$ and $x = -2$

B. $x = \frac{1}{2}$ and $x = 2$

C. $x = \frac{1}{2}$ and $x = 1$

D. $x = \frac{1}{2}$ and $x = -2$

E. $x = -\frac{1}{2}$ and $x = -2$

Question 3:

Evaluate the following sum:

$$\sum_{n=0}^{4} 3^{-n}$$

A. $\frac{112}{81}$

B. $\frac{121}{81}$

C. $\frac{121}{80}$

D. $\frac{120}{81}$

E. $\frac{121}{41}$

Question 4:

If $\dfrac{\log_2 8^x}{\log_3 9^y} = 12$ and $3x + 5y = 10$, what is x?

A. $\frac{80}{29}$

B. $\frac{80}{22}$

C. $\frac{60}{29}$

D. $\frac{40}{29}$

E. $\frac{80}{28}$

~ 25 ~

Question 5:

Evaluate the following integral:

$$\int_0^5 \frac{6x}{3x^2 + 5}\,dx$$

A. $\ln(10)$ C. $\ln(16)$ E. $-\ln(20)$

B. $\ln(12)$ D. $-\ln(16)$

Question 6:

What is the equation of the following graph?

A. $y = x^2 - 8$
B. $y = 2x^2 + 8$
C. $y = 2x^2 - 8$
D. $y = 2x^2 - 6$
E. $y = x^2 + 8$

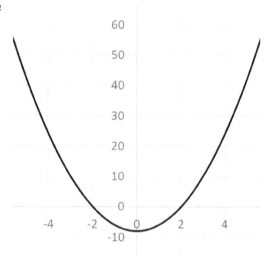

Question 7:

How does the gravitational field strength at the equator differ from the field strength at the north pole?

A. Weaker than at the north pole.
B. Stronger than at the north pole.
C. The same.
D. Twice as strong as at the north pole.
E. Not enough information.

Question 8:

A radio transmitter emits a radio signal with frequency of 1 MHz. What is the wavelength of the signal?

A. 600 m   C. 250 m   E. 300 m
B. 150 m   D. 200 m

Question 9:

What is the overall resistance of the following circuit?

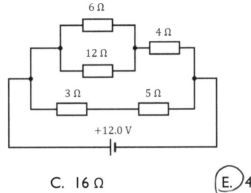

A. 12 Ω   C. 16 Ω   E. 4 Ω
B. 10 Ω   D. 8 Ω

Question 10:

A capacitor with a capacitance of 4.7 µF is used to store charge from a 25 V battery. If the fully charged capacitor is later used to power an LED with a constant current of 5 mA, for how long will the LED light up?

A. 0.02 s   C. 0.4 s   E. 0.1 s
B. 0.2 s   D. 0.01 s

Question 11:

Consider the system below. If a point force F is placed at $x = 3$ m, what is the value of F needed to keep the balance level?

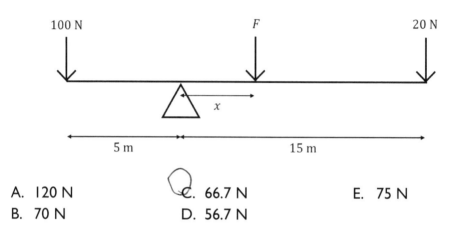

100 N F 20 N

x

5 m   15 m

A. 120 N   C. 66.7 N   E. 75 N

B. 70 N   D. 56.7 N

Question 12:

A particle of mass m and charge q is accelerated from rest under a potential difference V. The particle then hits a metal plate and rebounds, with no energy loss. If the direction of the particle's travel before it hits the wall is defined as positive, what is the change in momentum of the particle during the collision?

A. $2\sqrt{2Vqm}$ C. $-2\sqrt{2Vqm}$ E. $3\sqrt{2Vqm}$

B. $\sqrt{2Vqm}$ D. $-\sqrt{2Vqm}$

Question 13:

Expand $(5 - 3x)^4$ as a sum of powers of x.

$625 - 1500x + 1350x^2 - 540x^3 + 81x^4$

Question 14:

Andy throws a fair dice three times. What is the probability that

    a) all three throws give an even number, $1/6$

    b) all three throws give a prime number,

    c) the sum of the three throws is greater than or equal to 15?

Question 15:
A spring with spring constant k and natural length L is used to support a block of mass m. Another spring system consisting of two of the above springs in parallel is used to support the same mass. What is the extension of this parallel spring system?

$\frac{mg}{2k}$

Question 16:
A box has width equal to a sphere's radius r. The height of the box is half its length. If the volume of the box is twice the volume of the sphere, what are the full dimensions of the box?

$\frac{16}{3}\pi r \times r \times \frac{1}{2}r$

Question 17:
A car travelling on a motorway experiences air resistance, the force of which is proportional to the car's velocity, i.e. $R = -\alpha v$ where R is the air resistance in N and v is the car's velocity in ms⁻¹. The engine of the car produces a constant driving force F.
 a) What is the equation of motion of the car?
 b) What are the SI units of α?
 c) Calculate the terminal velocity of the car.

Question 18:
Two waves with the same speed, amplitude and wavelength λ are transmitted at the same time from two different points as shown in the diagram below.

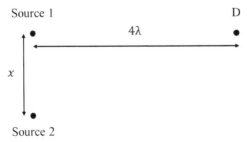

What must x be for the detector at D to detect:
 a) minimum interference, or
 b) maximum interference?

Question 19:

For $0 \le x \le 2\pi$, what is the solution to the following equations?

    a) $\sin x \cos x = \dfrac{1}{2}$

    b) $\sin^2 x - \cos^2 x = 0$ 45,315

Question 20:

A planet of mass m is located between two stars of masses M_1 and M_2, separated by a distance L as shown in the diagram below. Find an expression for the acceleration, a, of the planet in terms of the distance x between the planet and M_1.

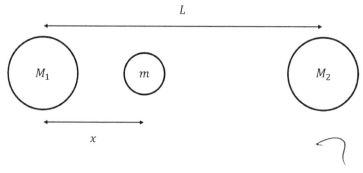

Question 21:

Evaluate the following integral:

$$\frac{d}{dt} \int_0^{3t} x^3 t^2 \, dx$$

Question 22:

A circle is given by the equation $(x - 5)^2 + (y + 3)^2 - 25 = 0$. What is the equation of the tangent to the circle at the point (8, 1)?

$-\dfrac{3}{4}, x + 7 = y$

END OF PAPER

Mock Paper B

Question 1:
What is the coefficient of x^6 in the expansion of $(1 - 2x)^3 (2 + x)^4$?

A. 54   B. -54 C. -52 D. -50 E. 50

Question 2:
Solve the following equation for x:

$$\log_3 x^2 + \log_4 \frac{1}{64} = 3$$

A. 18   B. 21   C. 27   D. 30   E. 33

Question 3:
Differentiate $y = 5x^2 \tan \left(\frac{1}{2}x + 3 \right)$ with respect to x.

A. $10x \tan \left(\frac{1}{2}x + 3 \right) - \frac{5}{2}x^2 \sec^2 \left(\frac{1}{2}x + 3 \right)$

B. $10x \tan \left(\frac{1}{2}x + 3 \right) + \frac{5}{2}x^2 \sec^2 \left(\frac{1}{2}x + 3 \right)$

C. $5x \tan \left(\frac{1}{2}x + 3 \right) + \frac{5}{2}x^2 \sec^2 \left(\frac{1}{2}x + 3 \right)$

D. $5x \tan \left(\frac{1}{2}x + 3 \right) + 5x^2 \sec^2 \left(\frac{1}{2}x + 3 \right)$

E. $10x \tan \left(\frac{1}{2}x + 3 \right) - \frac{5}{2}x^2 \sec^2 \left(\frac{1}{2}x + 3 \right)$

Question 4:
What is the equation of the line that connects the points (-3, 5) and (2, -6)?

A. $5y + 11x = 8$ D. $5y + 11x = -8$
B. $-5y + 11x = -8$ E. $5y - 11x = 8$
C. $5y - 11x = -8$

Question 5:
Evaluate the sum of the following series: 1 + 3 + 5 + ... + 99.

A. 1500   B. 2000   C. 2250   D. 2500   E. 2750

Question 6:
How many numbers greater than 3000 may be formed by using some or all of the digits 1, 2, 3, 4, and 5 without repetition?

A. 144   B. 160   C. 176   D. 188   E. 192

Question 7:
Which of the following statements is/are correct regarding our solar system?
   i.   The smallest planet is Mercury and the biggest planet is Jupiter.
   ii.   Jupiter has more moons than Saturn.
   iii. Mercury is the only planet without moons.
   iv.   As the mean distance from the Sun increases, the duration of the year on each planet increases.
   v.   As the mean distance from the Sun increases, the duration of the day on each planet increases.

 A. i, iv   C. i, ii   E. i, iii, v
B. i, ii, iv   D. ii, iv

Question 8:
In which part of the electromagnetic spectrum do waves have a wavelength of approximately 100 nm?

A. Visible   C. Ultraviolet   E. Microwave
B. Infrared   D. Gamma ray

Question 9:
What is the overall resistance of the following circuit?

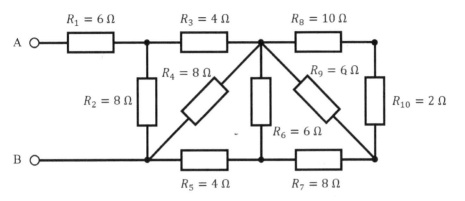

A. 4 Ω
B. 8 Ω

C. 10 Ω
D. 12 Ω

E. 14 Ω

Question 10:
Two satellites are in orbit around Earth. The first is in a geostationary orbit, whilst the second satellite orbits at a radius equal to a quarter of that of the first. What is the (approximate) period, in hours, of the second satellite?

A. 2½ hours
B. 24 hours

C. 8 hours
D. 3 hours

E. 5 hours

Question 11:
A radioactive sample A has a half-life of 3 days. How long does it take until the remaining amount is $\frac{1}{64}$ of the initial amount?

A. 9 days
B. 12 days

C. 18 days
D. 24 days

E. 30 days

Question 12:

A cube has sides of length of x cm. If the cube is cut into 64 identical smaller cubes, what is the total surface area of all the smaller cubes combined?

A. $16x^2$ cm^2 C. $30x^2$ cm^2 E. $64x^2$ cm^2

B. $24x^2$ cm^2 D. $36x^2$ cm^2

Question 13:

A fair dice is thrown 3 times. What is the probability that

a) there are two odd numbers and one even number,
b) exactly one six is thrown, $\frac{2}{2}16$
c) the largest number of the three throws is 3?

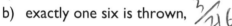

Question 14:

An arrow of mass 100 g is fired from the top of a cliff of height 20 m at a speed of 30 ms^{-1} and at an angle of 30° to the horizontal. How far (horizontally) from the cliff will the arrow be when it lands in the sea? Assume there is no air resistance. $68.9m$

Question 15:

What is the sum of the following terms?
$$1 - e^{-2x} + e^{-4x} + \cdots$$
Over what range of x is the solution valid?

Question 16:

Evaluate the following integrals:

a) $\int_0^{\frac{\pi}{2}} \frac{\sin x}{1 + \cos x} dx$

b) $\int_0^3 \frac{x^2}{2x^3 + 8} dx$

Question 17:

Given the circuit below, where all resistors have the same resistance R, what is:

a) the total resistance of the circuit?

b) the potential difference between A and B?

$\Delta v \quad \dfrac{2+4}{v}$

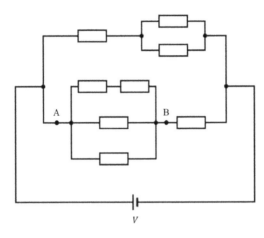

Question 18:

A field in the shape of a regular hexagon of side 5 m is used to grow corn. If each corn plant requires an area of $\dfrac{\sqrt{3}}{4}$ m^2, how many plants can be grown at the same time?

Question 19:

A sphere of radius r has twice the volume of a cone with the same base radius. Express the surface area of the cone in terms of r.

$\pi r \left(r + \sqrt{\frac{1}{2}h^2 + 1^2} \right)$

Question 20:

Sketch the region defined by the following inequalities:

$$x \geq 0$$
$$0 \leq y \leq 5$$
$$y \geq 2x + 1$$
$$y \geq \frac{1}{x}$$

Evaluate the area defined by the above inequalities.

Question 21:

Find the equation of the tangent to the circle $x^2 + y^2 = 25$ at (-3, 4).

$$4 \; g - 3n = 25$$

Question 22:

Two masses m_1 and m_2 are connected by a massless, non-extensible string supported by a smooth, massless pulley attached to the edge of a sloped surface inclined at an angle θ, as shown in the figure below. Assuming no friction, derive an expression for the acceleration of the masses and for the tension of the string.

$$m_1 g - T = m_1 a$$
$$T - m_2 g \sin \theta = m_2 \sin \theta \, a$$

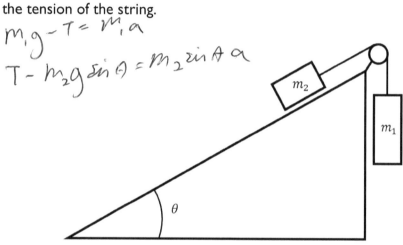

Now consider friction acting on the surface, with coefficient of static friction μ_s and coefficient of dynamic friction μ_d. What condition needs to be satisfied for:

$\mu_s R \; must \; be \cdot equal \; to$

a) m_2 to stay at rest, $m_2 g - m g$

b) m_2 to accelerate? $m_1 g - T \; must \; be \; greater \; than \; m_2 g$

For case b), derive expressions for the acceleration of the masses and for the tension of the string.

END OF PAPER

Mock Paper C

Question 1:

What is the coefficient of x^3 in the expansion of $(2-x)^2(2+x)^4(x-2)^2$?

A. 16   B. 8   C. 0   D. -8   E. -16

Question 2:

Evaluate the following integral:

$$\int_3^4 \frac{1}{x^2+x-6}dx$$

A. $0.2\ln\left(\frac{12}{7}\right)$ C. $-0.2\ln\left(\frac{12}{14}\right)$ E. $-0.2\ln\left(\frac{12}{9}\right)$

B. $0.2\ln\left(\frac{12}{14}\right)$ D. $0.2\ln\left(\frac{6}{7}\right)$

Question 3:

What is the second derivative of $f(x) = e^{-2x} + x^2$?

A. $4e^{-2x} + 2$ C. $2e^{-2x} + 2$ E. $2e^{-2x} - 2$

B. $4e^{-2x} - 2$ D. $e^{-2x} + 2$

Question 4:

Find the equation of the tangent to the curve $y = 3x^2$ at the point $(1, 3)$.

A. $y = 6x + 3$ C. $y = 6x - 6$ E. $y = -6x + 3$

B. $y = 3x - 3$ D. $y = 6x - 3$

~ 37 ~

Question 5:

Differentiate $y = \frac{\sin(2x+5)}{x^2+6x}$ with respect to x.

A. $\frac{2(\cos(2x+5))(x^2+6x)-(2x+6)\sin(2x+5)}{(x^2-6x)^2}$

B. $\frac{2(\cos(2x+5))(x^2+6x)+(2x+6)\sin(2x+5)}{(x^2+6x)^2}$

C. $\frac{2(\cos(2x+5))(x^2+6x)-(2x+6)\sin(2x+5)}{(x^2+6x)^2}$

D. $\frac{2(\sin(2x+5))(x^2+6x)-(2x+6)\sin(2x+5)}{(x^2+6x)^2}$

E. $\frac{2(\cos(2x+5))(x^2+6x)-(2x+6)\cos(2x+5)}{(x^2+6x)^2}$

Question 6:

Evaluate the following sum:

$$1 + \frac{1}{2} + \frac{1}{4} + \cdots$$

A. 1.75   B. 2   C. 2.25   D. 2.5   E. 3

Question 7:

What is the approximate gravitational acceleration at the surface of the moon? Assume that the densities of the moon and earth are equal and that the radius of the moon is 3.5 times smaller than the radius of earth.

A. 1.8 ms^{-2} C. 2.5 ms^{-2} E. 3.3 ms^{-2}

B. 2.0 ms^{-2} D. 2.9 ms^{-2}

Question 8:

What is the average separation of molecules of an ideal gas at atmospheric pressure ($\sim 10^5$ Pa) and room temperature ($\sim 25\ °C$)?
Avogadro's constant is $N_A = 6.022 \times 10^{23}$ mol^{-1}.

A. 3.5×10^{-9} m
B. 4.5×10^{-9} m

C. 5.5×10^{-9} m
D. 6.5×10^{-9} m
E. 7.5×10^{-9} m

Question 9:

Given that all the resistors have the same resistance R, what is the total resistance of the circuit below?

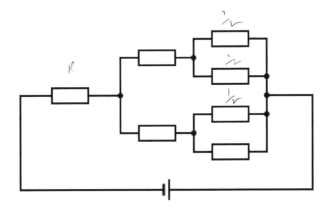

A. $\dfrac{7R}{16}$

B. $\dfrac{7R}{8}$

C. $\dfrac{7R}{4}$

D. $\dfrac{7R}{2}$

E. $7R$

Question 10:

Which of the following statements is/are correct about a satellite that is in a geostationary orbit?

 i. The satellite always appears to stay in one place in the sky to someone on Earth.

 ii. It can only be achieved above the equator.

 iii. It has a period of 12 hours.

 iv. It is moving in the opposite direction to earth's rotation.

 v. It enables antenna on earth to be pointed permanently at a fixed position in the sky.

A. i and ii

B. ii and iv

C. ii and v

D. i, ii, v

E. i, iii, v

Question 11:

What is the correct order of visible light, from shortest to longest wavelength?

A. violet-blue-green-yellow-orange-red
B. violet-blue-yellow-green-orange-red
C. red-orange-yellow-green-blue-violet
D. red-green-orange-yellow-blue-violet
E. green-red-yellow-orange-blue-violet

Question 12:

A radioactive sample A has a half-life of 6 days. A different radioactive sample B has a half-life of 9 days. Initially there is twice as much of A as of B. What is the ratio of A:B after 36 days?

A. 3:2   B. 2:1   C. 1:4   D. 1:1   E. 1:2

Question 13:

Evaluate the following integral:

$$\int_0^{0.5} (1 + q + q^2 + \cdots + q^N)\, dq$$

where $0 \leq q < 1$ and N is large.

Question 14:

The shape below consists of a square with sides of length r and four semicircles, each with radius $\frac{r}{2}$. What is the area of the shaded region?

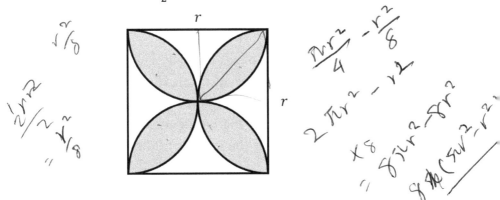

Question 15:

A golfer swings a club so that the head completes a full circle in 0.1 s. The length of the club is 1 m. Ignoring air resistance and assuming that the mass of the ball is negligible, estimate the maximum distance the golfer could hit the ball.

HINT: Consider the optimal angle at which the golfer should hit the ball.

Question 16:

A ball of mass 50 g is attached to a spring that can be extended by a length of 10 cm. If the maximum speed of the ball is 15 ms^{-1}, what is the upper limit on the spring constant? Discuss whether this limit would be different on the Moon.

Question 17:

A box contains flowers of five different colours. There are twice as many yellow as green, three times as many red as yellow, four times as many blue as red, and five times as many purple as blue. Only one flower is taken at a time and replaced before selecting the next one. What is the probability of taking

a) a yellow flower,
b) a red flower,
c) a purple flower?

Question 18:

The interior of a planetarium needs painting. The wall of the planetarium is in the form of a hollow cylinder of radius R and height h. The ceiling of the planetarium is a hemisphere that sits right on top of the walls. If the layer of paint on the walls and the ceiling must have a thickness t, how much paint is required to paint the interior of the planetarium?

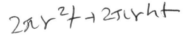

Question 19:

Sketch the region defined by the following inequalities and evaluate its area:

$$x^2 + 1 \geq y$$
$$y \geq -1$$
$$0 \leq x \leq 1$$

Question 20:

A block of mass m is pulled, via a pulley, along a surface inclined at angle θ. The coefficients of static and kinetic friction between the block and the surface are μ_s and μ_k respectively. Determine the force F when the block is a) at rest; b) moving at constant velocity.

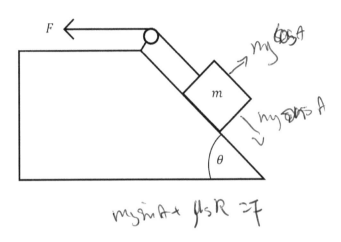

Question 21:

Sketch the path of light travelling from a medium of optical density n_1 into a medium of optical density n_2, where $n_1 > n_2$. Label the angle of incidence (θ_1) and the angle of refraction (θ_2). Using Snell's law, derive the relationship between the critical angle (θ_c) and the angle of incidence.

Carbon disulphide liquid ($n = 1.63$) is poured into a container made of crown glass ($n = 1.52$). What is the critical angle for internal reflection of a ray in the liquid when it is incident on the liquid-to-glass surface?

END OF PAPER

Mock Paper D

Question 1:
Find the roots of the equation $x^3 - 7x + 6 = 0$ by factorising it.

A. 3, 2, and -1

B. 3, 2, and 1

C. -3, 2, and 1

D. 3, -2, and 1

E. -3, -2, and -1

Question 2:
Find the derivative of $f(x) = 2\cos x + x^2$.

A. $2\sin x + 2x$

B. $-2\sin x + 2x$

C. $-2\sin x - 2x$

D. $-2\cos x + 2x$

E. $2\cos x + 2x$

Question 3:
If a 1000 km tall skyscraper was built, what would be the ratio of your weight at the top of it to your weight on the ground? The radius of Earth is 6371 km.

A. $\dfrac{6371^2}{7371^2}$

B. $\dfrac{6370^2}{7370^2}$

C. $\dfrac{7370^2}{6370^2}$

D. $\dfrac{6370}{7370}$

E. $\dfrac{6371}{7371}$

Question 4:
A ball of mass m is attached to two springs of spring constant k connected in parallel that can be extended by a length L. What is the maximum speed of the ball during oscillations?

A. $\sqrt{\dfrac{k}{m}}\,L$

B. $\sqrt{\dfrac{k}{2m}}\,L$

C. $\sqrt{\dfrac{2k}{m}}\,L$

D. $\sqrt{\dfrac{k}{m^2}}\,L$

E. $\sqrt{\dfrac{k^2}{2m}}\,L$

Question 5:
At constant pressure, an ideal monoatomic gas is compressed to half its original volume. If the original temperature of the gas was T_1, find an expression for its final temperature.

A. T_1 B. $\frac{1}{2}T_1$ C. $\frac{1}{4}T_1$ D. $2T_1$ E. $\frac{1}{8}T_1$

Question 6:
A ray of light travelling through the air is incident at an angle of 60° to a layer of water. It then travels through the layer of water ($n = 1.34$) until it reaches a layer of oil ($n = 1.55$). Find the angle of refraction at the water-oil boundary.

A. 60°   B. 55°   C. 45°   D. 42°   E. 34°

Question 7:
What is the equation of the tangent to the curve $y = \sqrt{8x - 4x^2}$ at the point $x = 2$?

A. $x = 2$ C. $y = 2x$ E. $y = -2$
B. $y = 2$ D. $y = 2x + 2$

Question 8:
The three roots of a third order polynomial are -1, 0 and 1. Which of the following could be an expression for the polynomial?

A. $x^3 - x + 1$ C. $x^3 + x$ E. $x^3 - x - 6$
B. $x^3 - 2x - 3$ D. $x^3 - x$

Question 9:
Find the area enclosed by the curves $y = x^2$ and $y = x$.

A. $\frac{1}{6}$ B. $\frac{1}{4}$ C. $\frac{1}{2}$ D. $\frac{1}{8}$ E. $\frac{1}{12}$

Question 10:

If the radius of Earth was double its current value but assuming its mass was the same, what would the gravitational acceleration at Earth's surface be?

A. 1.25 ms^{-2} C. 5.0 ms^{-2} E. 15 ms^{-2}

B. 2.5 ms^{-2} D. 10.0 ms^{-2}

Question 11:

Which of the following statements is/are correct about electromagnetic waves?

  i.   Infrared waves have a longer wavelength than visible light.
  ii. X-rays have the shortest wavelength and radio waves have the longest.
  iii. The wavelength of ultraviolet light varies from 10-400 nm.
  iv. A wave with a frequency of 1 GHz must be a radio wave.
  v.   Red light has a higher frequency than violet light.

A. i and iii   C. i and iv   E. i, iii, iv

B. i and ii   D. i, iii, v

Question 12:

A bullet of mass 100 g travelling at a speed of 100 ms^{-1} hits a stationary wrecking ball of mass 2 kg. If the bullet and ball combine, what will be the speed of the combined object immediately after the collision?

A. 1.8 ms^{-1} C. 3.8 ms^{-1} E. 5.8 ms^{-1}

B. 2.8 ms^{-1} D. 4.8 ms^{-1}

Question 13:

Evaluate the following integrals:

a) $\displaystyle\int_{-\pi/2}^{\pi/2} \sin(x)\cos(x)\,dx$

b) $\int \left(x^2 e^{x^3} + \sin^2 x\right) dx$

Question 14:

You want to build a snowman in a garden of dimensions 20 m × 20 m. You can only use the snow in the garden. The thickness of the snow layer is 5 cm. The snowman consists of three spheres of radii R, $1.5R$ and $2R$. What is the largest possible value of R?

Sasha

$0.505m$

Question 15:

In a basket there are green apples, red apples, green pears and red pears. There are $2x - 1$ green apples, $x + 2$ red apples and $x - 3$ green pears. There are also twice as many red pears as green pears in the basket. What is the probability of taking from the basket

a) an apple,

b) a piece of green fruit,

c) a red pear?

a) $\dfrac{3x(-3)}{6x(-8)}$

b) $\dfrac{3x-4}{6x-8} = \dfrac{1}{2}$

c) $\dfrac{2x-6}{6x-8}$

Question 16:

The shape below consists of three circles and a line that splits each circle in two. If the diameter of the largest circle is 8 and the diameters of the inner circles are 5 and 3, what is the area of the shaded region?

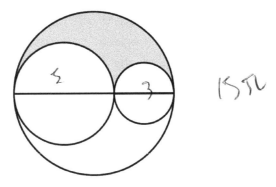

15π

Question 17:

Sketch the lines $y = 2x$ and $2x = -y + 4$. Find the area enclosed by these lines and the x-axis.

2

Question 18:

The diagram below shows a system of two smooth pulleys, where all strings are massless and inextensible. Find expressions for the accelerations of the masses m_1, m_2 and m_3. You do not need to simplify the expressions.

$$a = \frac{(m_2 + m_3 - m_1)g}{m_1 + m_2 + m_3}$$

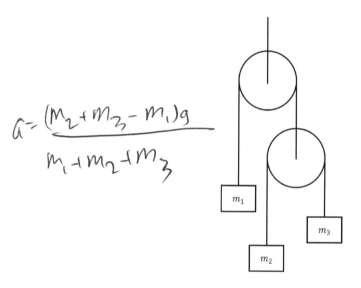

Question 19:

A cannon shoots a ball at an angle of 30° to the horizontal. If the range of the cannon is $D = 100$ m (neglecting air resistance), what is the initial speed of the ball? Keeping the initial speed constant, what simple modification could you make to improve the range of the cannon?

increase launch angle to 45°

$$u = \left(\frac{2000g}{\sqrt{3}}\right)^{\frac{1}{2}}$$

Question 20:

A cable car of mass 200 kg and slope 30° is used to raise passengers from point A to point B. The difference in height between point A and point B is 400 m. If the friction coefficient between the cable and the cable car is 0.02, and the efficiency of the electric motor of the cable car is 0.1, calculate the total energy required to raise a group of passengers of total mass 300 kg from point A to point B in the cable car. If this ride lasts 2 minutes, calculate the power of the engine.

Question 21:

Consider the circuit diagram below, where all resistors are identical and have resistance R. What is the potential difference between the following nodes? qv

a) Point A and Point B

b) Point A and Point C

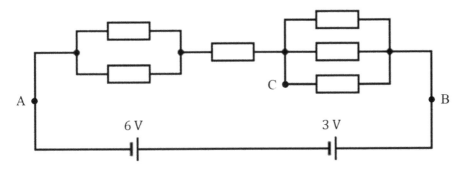

Question 22:

Three point charges, $+q$, $+q$ and $-q$, are attached to the vertices of an equilateral triangle of side length a. What is the electric field at the centre of the triangle? What would the electric field at the centre be if all three charges had the same sign?

END OF PAPER

Mock Paper E

Question 1:
Evaluate the following integral:

$$\int_3^4 \frac{2x - 1}{x^2 - x - 1}\,dx$$

A. $\ln\left(\frac{11}{8}\right)$
B. $\ln\left(\frac{11}{6}\right)$
C. $\ln\left(\frac{11}{5}\right)$
D. $\ln\left(\frac{22}{5}\right)$
E. $\ln\left(\frac{22}{13}\right)$

Question 2:
Differentiate $f(x) = \ln^2(x^2)$ with respect to x.

A. $\dfrac{4\ln(x^2)}{x}$
B. $\dfrac{2\ln(x^2)}{x}$
C. $\dfrac{4\ln(x^2)}{x^2}$
D. $\dfrac{-2\ln(x^2)}{x}$
E. $\dfrac{4\ln(x)}{x}$

Question 3:
Find r if:

$$\sum_{i=0}^{\infty} 5r^i = 10$$

A. $\dfrac{1}{6}$
B. $\dfrac{1}{3}$
C. $\dfrac{1}{8}$
D. $\dfrac{1}{4}$
E. $\dfrac{1}{2}$

Question 4:
Find x and y if $\log_2\left(\frac{x}{y}\right) = 3$ and $6y + x = 14$.

A. $y = 1$ and $x = 4$
B. $y = 1$ and $x = 8$
C. $y = 2$ and $x = 8$
D. $y = 2$ and $x = 4$
E. $y = 2$ and $x = 16$

Question 5:

A card is picked randomly from a complete deck of cards, excluding jokers. What is the probability that the card is red and has a prime number on it?

A. $\frac{2}{13}$　　　B. $\frac{3}{13}$　　　C. $\frac{4}{13}$　　　D. $\frac{5}{13}$　　　E. $\frac{6}{13}$

Question 6:

What is the equation of the following graph?

A. $y = x^2 - 6x + 6$
B. $y = 2x^2 + 12x + 12$
C. $y = 2x^2 - 12x + 18$
D. $y = 2x^2 - 12x + 12$
E. $y = x^2 - 13x + 12$

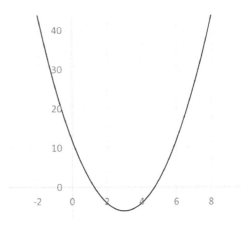

Question 7:

What would the gravitational acceleration at the Earth's surface be if the Earth's density was double its current value, but its radius remained the same?

A. 9.8 ms^{-2}　　　　C. 39.2 ms^{-2}　　　　E. 2.45 ms^{-2}
B. 19.6 ms^{-2}　　　　D. 4.9 ms^{-2}

Question 8:

An ideal monoatomic gas of mass m and molecular weight M is stored in a cube of side length a at constant temperature T. What is the total force exerted by the gas on the cube?

A. $\dfrac{8\left(\frac{m}{M}\right)RT}{a}$

C. $\dfrac{4\left(\frac{m}{M}\right)RT}{a}$

E. $\dfrac{3\left(\frac{m}{M}\right)RT}{a}$

B. $\dfrac{6\left(\frac{m}{M}\right)RT}{a}$

D. $\dfrac{3\left(\frac{m}{M}\right)RT}{2a}$

Question 9:

A battery with emf 1.5 V and internal resistance of 0.1 Ω is connected to a fixed resistor of resistance R Ω. If the current drawn is measured to be 0.5 A, what is the value of R?

A. 5.9 Ω   B. 4.9 Ω   C. 3.9 Ω   D. 2.9 Ω   E. 1.9 Ω

Question 10:

In a multi-planetary system, two planets (A and B) orbit around star S. The mean distance from planet A to star S is 2 AU, whereas the mean distance from planet B to star S is 8 AU. If planet A has an orbital period of 1000 days, what is the orbital period of planet B?

A. 8000 days

C. 2000 days

E. 500 days

B. 4000 days

D. 1000 days

Question 11:

A capacitor with capacitance 30 nF is charged using a 1.5 V battery. If the fully charged capacitor is then used to power an LED with a constant current of 2 μA, how long will the LED be on for?

A. 22.5 s

C. 0.225 s

E. 22.5 ms

B. 2.25 s

D. 25 ms

Question 12:
A car of mass 100 kg is travelling at a speed of 72 km/h when the driver sees a red light 100 m in front of the car. What is the average braking force required so that the car fully stops just before the red light? Ignore air resistance.

A. 200 N
B. 299 N

C. 350 N
D. 450 N

E. 750 N

Question 13:
A pool of width 20 m and length 50 m is being filled with water. The minimum depth of the pool is 1.5 m. It is shallowest along one of its shorter sides and deepest along the other short side, with a constant angle of inclination of 3°. If 1 litre of water per square metre evaporates from the surface of the pool every hour, calculate the total amount of water required to fill the pool and keep it full for a week.

Question 14:
There are twice as many cod as trout in a fishpond, and three times as many trout as salmon. Only fish heavier than 2 kg are kept. If every second cod, every third trout and every fourth salmon are lighter than 2 kg, what is the probability of catching:
   a) a trout heavier than 2 kg,
   b) a salmon lighter than 2 kg,
   c) any fish heavier than 2 kg?

Question 15:

The length of both legs (catheti) of the right-angled triangle shown below is 2. If the circle is centred at the middle of one of the triangle's legs, what is the area of the shaded region?

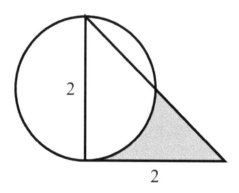

Question 16:

Evaluate the following integrals:

a) $\int (1 + e^{-2x}) \sin(2x - e^{-2x}) \, dx$

b) $\int \dfrac{3x - 5}{(x - 3)(x^2 - 3x + 2)} \, dx$

Question 17:

Polar coordinates are an alternative coordinate system to Cartesian coordinates, where r represents the length of a line connecting a point to the origin, and θ gives the angle between this line and the x-axis. This alternative system is illustrated in the diagram below:

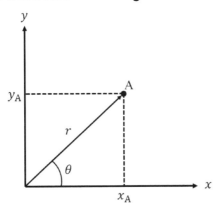

Hence, transform the equation

$$r^2 \cos^2 \theta - 2r \cos \theta + r^2 \sin^2 \theta = 24$$

from polar (r, θ) to Cartesian (x, y) coordinates. Sketch the resulting graph.

Question 18:

A ball of mass m is attached to a spring of spring constant k_1, that is itself attached to a spring of spring constant k_2 $(k_2 < k_1)$. If each of the springs can be extended by a length l before breaking, determine the maximum speed of the ball.

Question 19:

Consider the circuit below, where the transformer has N_1 turns on its primary coil, and N_2 turns on its secondary coil.

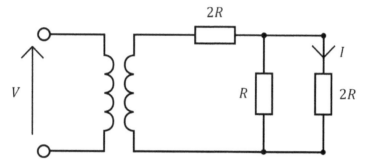

Find an expression for the current, I, in terms of V, R, N_P and N_S.

Question 20:

A sphere of radius R is non-uniformly charged. The density of the charge, ρ, varies as:

$$\rho = ar; \text{ when } r < R \ (a \text{ is constant})$$
$$\rho = 0; \text{ when } r > R$$

Determine how the magnitude of the electric field inside and outside the sphere changes with the distance r from the centre of the sphere.

Question 21:

A rocket accelerates vertically upwards with an acceleration of $2g$. The wind blows upwards with a speed of w ms^{-1} at an angle of α to the horizontal. Assume that the initial velocity of the rocket immediately after take-off is equal to the wind velocity. Assuming that there are no losses in the interaction of the wind and the rocket, determine the total horizontal displacement of the rocket when it reaches a height of H km.

Question 22:

Consider the diagram below, where a mass m_1 rests on top of another mass m_2, which itself sits on plane inclined at an angle α. If the friction coefficient between m_1 and m_2 is μ_1 and the friction coefficient between m_2 and the inclined plane is μ_2, determine:

a) the acceleration of m_2,
b) the acceleration of m_1 with respect to the plane,
c) the acceleration of m_1 with respect to m_2.

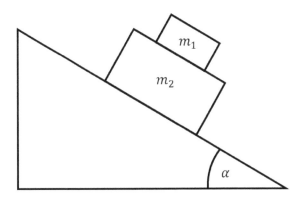

Question 23

An aeroplane of mass 3000 kg is raised to a height of 11 km by its engine. The plane's average speed is 900 km/h and the air resistance experienced is given by $F = kv^2$ where $k = 10^{-3}\,\text{Ns}^2\text{m}^{-2}$. Ignoring the time taken for the plane to rise to the height of 11 km and neglecting the losses due to air resistance on the ascent and descent, how much energy would be required to travel from London to Glasgow (a straight horizontal distance of 556 km)?

END OF PAPER

ANSWERS

Mock Paper A Answers

Question 1: B

Use the product rule:

$$\frac{d}{dx}(f(x)g(x)) = f(x)\frac{dg(x)}{dx} + g(x)\frac{df(x)}{dx}$$

with $f(x) = 5x^2$ and $g(x) = \sin 2x$ in this case. Hence

$$\frac{d}{dx}(f(x)g(x)) = (5x^2)(2\cos 2x) + (\sin 2x)(10x)$$

$$= 10x(x\cos 2x + \sin 2x)$$

Question 2: D

If $x = 1$ is a root, then $(x - 1)$ is a factor. If we factorise $(x - 1)$ out of the polynomial we get:

$$2x^3 + x^2 - 5x = -2$$
$$2x^3 + x^2 - 5x + 2 = 0$$
$$(x - 1)(2x^2 + 3x - 2) = 0$$
$$(x - 1)(2x - 1)(x + 2) = 0$$

Hence, the other two roots are $x = \frac{1}{2}$ and $x = -2$.

Question 3: B

Expanding this sum gives $3^{-0} + 3^{-1} + 3^{-2} + 3^{-3} + 3^{-4}$. This is a geometric progression with first term 1 and common ratio $\frac{1}{3}$. There are 5 terms in total, hence

$$S_5 = \frac{a(r^5 - 1)}{r - 1} = \frac{1\left(\left(\frac{1}{3}\right)^5 - 1\right)}{1/3 - 1} = \frac{121}{81}$$

Question 4: A

Rearrange the first equation:

$$\frac{\log_2 8^x}{\log_3 9^y} = 12$$

$$\frac{x \log_2 8}{y \log_3 9} = 12$$

$$\frac{3x}{2y} = 12$$

$$x = 8y$$

Substitute this into the second equation:

$$3(8y) + 5y = 10$$

$$y = \frac{10}{29} \text{ and therefore } x = 8\left(\frac{10}{29}\right) = \frac{80}{29}$$

Question 5: C

Let $u = 3x^2 + 5$, then $\frac{du}{dx} = 6x$. Substitute u and du into the integral:

$$\int_0^5 \frac{6x}{3x^2 + 5} dx = \int_{x=0}^{x=5} \frac{1}{u} du$$

$$= [\ln u]_{x=0}^{x=5}$$

$$= [\ln(3x^2 + 5)]_0^5$$

$$= \ln(80) - \ln(5)$$

$$= \ln\left(\frac{80}{5}\right)$$

$$= \ln(16)$$

Question 6: C

The available options are all second order polynomials, hence the equation must be of the form

$$y = ax^2 + bx + c$$

When $x = 0$:

$$a(0)^2 + b(0) + c = -8$$
$$\boldsymbol{c = -8}$$

When $x = 2$:

$$a(2)^2 + b(2) - 8 = 0$$
$$4a + 2b = 8 \ (1)$$

When $x = -2$:

$$a(-2)^2 + b(-2) - 8 = 0$$
$$4a - 2b = 8 \ (2)$$

$(1) - (2)$:

$$4b = 0$$
$$\boldsymbol{b = 0}$$

Substitute back into (1):

$$4a = 8$$
$$\boldsymbol{a = 2}$$

$$\therefore y = ax^2 + bx + c = \boldsymbol{2x^2 - 8}$$

Question 7: A

Gravitational field strength is defined mathematically as $g = \frac{GM}{r^2}$ where G is a constant, M is the mass of Earth and r is the distance between Earth's core and the point of interest.

As the earth is not quite a perfect sphere (the distance to the north pole from Earth's core is shorter than the distance to the equator) the gravitational field strength on the equator is weaker than that at the north pole.

Question 8: E

$$\lambda = \frac{c}{f}$$

Radio waves are part of the electromagnetic spectrum and hence have the same speed as the speed of light:

$$= \frac{3 \times 10^8}{10^6}$$
$$= 300 \text{ m}$$

Question 9: E

Break the resistors up into different blocks, as in the diagram below.

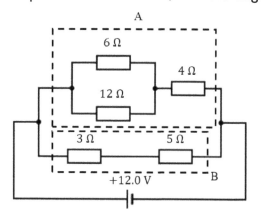

For block A:

$$R_A = 4 + \frac{(6)(12)}{6 + 12} = 8 \, \Omega$$

For block B:

$$R_B = 3 + 5 = 8 \, \Omega$$

The overall resistance is therefore

$$R_{total} = \frac{R_A R_B}{R_A + R_B}$$
$$= \frac{(8)(8)}{8 + 8}$$
$$= 4 \, \Omega$$

Question 10: A

Capacitance is defined as charge per unit voltage:

$$C = \frac{q}{V}$$
$$q = CV$$
$$= (4.7 \times 10^{-6})(25)$$
$$= 1.175 \times 10^{-4}\ C$$

Current is defined as charge per unit time:

$$I = \frac{q}{t}$$
$$t = \frac{q}{I}$$
$$= \frac{1.175 \times 10^{-4}}{5 \times 10^{-3}}$$
$$\approx \mathbf{0.02\ s}$$

Question 11: C

If the system is balanced, clockwise moment = anti-clockwise moment:

$$F(3) + 20(15) = 100(5)$$
$$F = \frac{500 - 300}{3}$$
$$= \frac{200}{3}$$
$$= \mathbf{66.7\ N}$$

Question 12: C

Assuming all kinetic energy is gained from electrical potential energy:

$$\frac{1}{2}mv_1^2 = Vq$$

$$v_1 = \sqrt{\frac{2Vq}{m}}$$

As the particle rebounds with no energy loss, its velocity after the collision will be the same magnitude but in the opposite direction: $v_2 = -\sqrt{\frac{2Vq}{m}}$. The change in momentum is therefore:

$$\Delta p = m(v_2 - v_1)$$

$$= m\left(-\sqrt{\frac{2Vq}{m}} - \sqrt{\frac{2Vq}{m}}\right)$$

$$= -2\sqrt{2Vqm}$$

Question 13

Using binomial expansion,

$$(5 - 3x)^4 = (5)^4 + 4(5)^3(-3x) + 6(5)^2(-3x)^2 + 4(5)(-3x)^3 + (-3x)^4$$

$$= 625 - 1500x + 1350x^2 - 540x^3 + 81x^4$$

Question 14

a) The even numbers are 2, 4, 6.

$$P(\text{even}) = \frac{3}{6} = \frac{1}{2}$$

Since the three throws are independent, the probabilities can be multiplied:

$$P(3 \text{ even numbers}) = \frac{1}{2} \times \frac{1}{2} \times \frac{1}{2} = \frac{1}{8}$$

b) The prime numbers are 2, 3, 5.

$$P(\text{prime}) = \frac{3}{6} = \frac{1}{2}$$

Similarly to part a),

$$P(3 \text{ prime numbers}) = \frac{1}{2} \times \frac{1}{2} \times \frac{1}{2} = \frac{1}{8}$$

c) Any combination where each number is either a 5 or 6 satisfies this condition, as well as the combinations (3, 6, 6), (4, 5, 6) and (4, 6, 6) in any order. All valid combinations are therefore shown in the table below.

1st Roll	2nd Roll	3rd Roll
3	6	6
4	5	6
	6	5, 6
5	4	6
	5	5, 6
	6	4, 5, 6
6	3	6
	4	5, 6
	5	4, 5, 6
	6	3, 4, 5, 6

Summing the total number of valid rolls in the table gives 20. Since there are $6^3 = 216$ possible rolls in total, the probability is

$$\frac{20}{216} = \frac{5}{54}$$

Question 15

If springs are used in parallel, their effective total spring constant is given by the sum of the individual spring constants, so $k_{total} = 2k$.

$$mg = k_{total}\, x$$
$$x = \frac{mg}{k_{total}} = \frac{mg}{2k}$$

Question 16

Let the dimensions of the box be $w \times h \times l$, where w, h and l are width, height and length respectively. There are three pieces of information about the box and three unknowns:

(1) $w = r$

(2) $h = \dfrac{l}{2}$

(3) $V = w \times h \times l = 2 \times \dfrac{4}{3}\pi r^3$

Substitute (1) and (2) into (3):

$$r \times \left(\frac{l}{2}\right) \times l = \frac{8}{3}\pi r^3$$
$$l^2 = \frac{16}{3}\pi r^2$$
$$l = 4\sqrt{\frac{\pi}{3}}\, r$$

Substitute back into (2):

$$h = 2\sqrt{\frac{\pi}{3}}\, r$$

So the full dimensions of the box are

$$r \times 2\sqrt{\frac{\pi}{3}}\, r \times 4\sqrt{\frac{\pi}{3}}\, r$$

Question 17

a) Newton's 2nd Law: $F - \alpha v = ma$.

b) As αv has the same dimensions as force (kgms^{-2} in SI units) and v is speed (ms^{-1}), then α must have units of **kgs^{-1}**.

c) Terminal velocity happens when the air resistance has reached a value such that there is zero acceleration:

$$F - \alpha v = 0$$
$$v = \frac{F}{\alpha}$$

Question 18

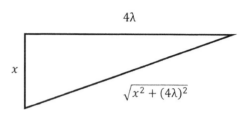

The path that waves from Source I travel along has length 4λ, whilst the path length from Source 2 to the detector is $\sqrt{x^2 + (4\lambda)^2}$.

a) For minimum (destructive) interference to happen, the path difference must be exactly a half number of wavelengths:

$$\left(n + \frac{1}{2}\right)\lambda = \sqrt{x^2 + (4\lambda)^2} - 4\lambda$$

$$\left(n + \frac{1}{2} + 4\right)\lambda = \sqrt{x^2 + (4\lambda)^2}$$

$$\left(n + \frac{9}{2}\right)^2 \lambda^2 = x^2 + 16\lambda^2$$

$$x^2 = \left(n + \frac{9}{2}\right)^2 \lambda^2 - 16\lambda^2$$

$$= \left(n^2 + 9n + \frac{81}{4} - 16\right)\lambda^2$$

$$= \left(n^2 + 9n + \frac{17}{4}\right)\lambda^2$$

$$\therefore x = \lambda \sqrt{n^2 + 9n + \frac{17}{4}}$$

where n is an integer (0, 1, 2, 3...)

b) For maximum (constructive) interference to happen, the path difference must be an exact number of wavelengths:

$$n\lambda = \sqrt{x^2 + (4\lambda)^2} - 4\lambda$$
$$(n + 4)\lambda = \sqrt{x^2 + (4\lambda)^2}$$
$$(n + 4)^2\lambda^2 = x^2 + 16\lambda^2$$
$$x^2 = (n^2 + 8n + 16 - 16)\lambda^2$$
$$\therefore x = \lambda\sqrt{n^2 + 8n}$$

Question 19

a) Using the $\sin 2x$ identity,

$$\sin x \cos x = \frac{1}{2}$$
$$\frac{\sin 2x}{2} = \frac{1}{2}$$
$$\sin 2x = 1$$
$$2x = \frac{\pi}{2}, \frac{5\pi}{2}$$
$$x = \frac{\pi}{4}, \frac{5\pi}{4}$$

b) Using the $\cos 2x$ identity,

$$\sin^2 x - \cos^2 x = 0$$
$$-\cos 2x = 0$$
$$\cos 2x = 0$$
$$2x = \frac{\pi}{2}, \frac{3\pi}{2}, \frac{5\pi}{2}, \frac{7\pi}{2}$$
$$x = \frac{\pi}{4}, \frac{3\pi}{4}, \frac{5\pi}{4}, \frac{7\pi}{4}$$

Question 20

The planet experiences a gravitational pull from both M_1 and M_2, the magnitude of which is given by the equation

$$F = \frac{GMm}{r^2}$$

$$M_1: F_1 = \frac{GM_1 m}{x^2}$$

$$M_2: F_2 = \frac{GM_2 m}{(L-x)^2}$$

Taking positive as rightwards:

$$\Sigma F = F_2 - F_1 = ma$$

$$a = \frac{F_2 - F_1}{m}$$

$$a = \frac{\dfrac{GM_2 m}{(L-x)^2} - \dfrac{GM_1 m}{x^2}}{m}$$

$$a = \frac{GM_2}{(L-x)^2} - \frac{GM_1}{x^2}$$

Question 21

Perform the integration as usual but be careful to substitute the limits of the integral in for the x values before differentiating.

$$\frac{d}{dt} \int_0^{3t} x^3 t^2 \, dx = \frac{d}{dt} \left[t^2 \left(\frac{x^4}{4} \right) \right]_{x=0}^{x=3t}$$

$$= \frac{d}{dt} \left(t^2 \left(\frac{(3t)^4}{4} \right) \right)$$

$$= \frac{d}{dt} \left(\frac{81}{4} t^6 \right)$$

$$= \frac{243}{2} t^5$$

Question 22

Using implicit differentiation,

$$\frac{d}{dx}(x-5)^2 + \frac{d}{dx}(y+3)^2 = \frac{d}{dx}(25)$$

$$2(x-5) + 2(y+3)\frac{dy}{dx} = 0$$

$$\frac{dy}{dx} = \frac{5-x}{y+3}$$

Substitute in the coordinates (8, 1):

$$\frac{dy}{dx}\bigg|_{x=8,y=1} = \frac{5-8}{1+3} = -\frac{3}{4}$$

Finally, use this value as the gradient of the tangent to find its equation:

$$y - y_1 = m(x - x_1)$$

$$y - 1 = -\frac{3}{4}(x - 8)$$

$$y = 1 - \frac{3}{4}x + 6$$

$$y = -\frac{3}{4}x + 7$$

END OF PAPER

Mock Paper B ANSWERS

Question 1: C
The x^6 term comes from $(x^2)(x^4)$ and $(x^3)(x^3)$ terms. Hence:
$$3(1)(-2x)^2(x^4) + (-2x)^3(4(2)(x)^3) = 12x^6 - 64x^6 = \mathbf{-52x^6}$$

Question 2: C
$$\log_4 \frac{1}{64} = \log_4 4^{-3} = -3$$
Hence,
$$\log_3 x^2 - 3 = 3$$
$$\log_3 x^2 = 6$$
$$x^2 = 3^6$$
$$= 729$$
$$\therefore x = 27$$

Question 3: B
$$y = 5x^2 \tan\left(\frac{1}{2}x + 3\right)$$
Use the product rule:
$$\frac{dy}{dx} = (10x) \tan\left(\frac{1}{2}x + 3\right) + (5x^2)\left(\frac{1}{2}\sec^2\left(\frac{1}{2}x + 3\right)\right)$$
$$= 10x \tan\left(\frac{1}{2}x + 3\right) + \frac{5}{2}x^2 \sec^2\left(\frac{1}{2}x + 3\right)$$

Question 4: D
The equation of the line can be obtained by:
$$y - y_1 = \left(\frac{y_2 - y_1}{x_2 - x_1}\right)(x - x_1)$$
$$y - 5 = \frac{-6 - 5}{2 - (-3)}(x - (-3))$$
$$= -\frac{11}{5}(x + 3)$$
$$\therefore 5y + 11x = -8$$

Question 5: D
This is an arithmetic series, with first term 1 and common difference $+2$.
We first need to find the nth term that is equal to **99**.

$$99 = 1 + (n - 1)2$$
$$n = 50$$

Hence,

$$S_{50} = \frac{n}{2}(2a + (n - 1)d)$$
$$= \frac{50}{2}(2 + 49 \times 2)$$
$$= \mathbf{2500}$$

Question 6: E
We can see that the numbers must be either 5 digits, when any combination is valid, or 4 digits, when the number must start with either 3, 4 or 5.

There are therefore $5 \times 4 \times 3 \times 2 \times 1 = 120$ possible 5-digit options, and $3 \times 4 \times 3 \times 2 = 72$ 4-digit options.

In total there are therefore
$$120 + 72 = \mathbf{192\ combinations}$$

Question 7: B
Statement (i) is correct. Jupiter has **67** moons in total whereas Saturn has **62** hence statement (ii) is correct. Venus also does not have any moons hence (iii) is incorrect. Statement (iv) is correct (Kepler's Third Law). Statement (v) is not necessarily correct as duration of day depends on rate of rotation which has no correlation with distance to Sun.

Question 8: C
Ultraviolet light has a typical wavelength range of $10 - 400$ nm.

Question 9: C

The easiest way to approach this question is by starting at the right-hand side of the circuit and simplifying the circuit stage by stage.

First, consider the diagram below:

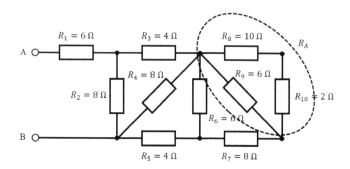

R_A is equivalent to R_8 and R_{10} in series, connected in parallel to R_9:

$$\frac{1}{R_A} = \frac{1}{R_9} + \frac{1}{R_8 + R_{10}}$$
$$= \frac{1}{6} + \frac{1}{12}$$
$$R_A = 4 \ \Omega$$

This gives the simplified circuit shown below:

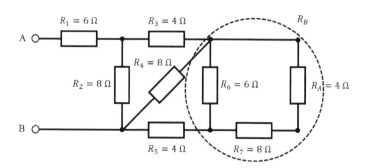

Similarly, R_B is equivalent to R_A and R_7 in series, connected in parallel with R_6:

$$\frac{1}{R_B} = \frac{1}{R_6} + \frac{1}{R_7 + R_A}$$
$$= \frac{1}{6} + \frac{1}{12}$$
$$R_B = 4\ \Omega$$

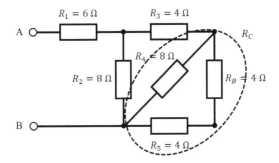

Similarly,

$$\frac{1}{R_C} = \frac{1}{R_4} + \frac{1}{R_5 + R_B}$$
$$= \frac{1}{8} + \frac{1}{8}$$
$$R_C = 4\ \Omega$$

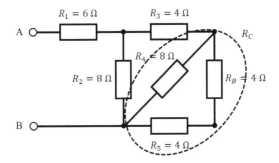

$$\frac{1}{R_D} = \frac{1}{R_2} + \frac{1}{R_3 + R_C}$$
$$= \frac{1}{8} + \frac{1}{8}$$
$$R_D = 4\ \Omega$$

Finally,

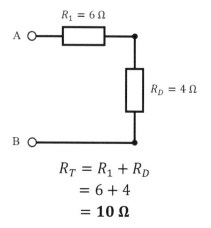

$$R_T = R_1 + R_D$$
$$= 6 + 4$$
$$= \mathbf{10\ \Omega}$$

Question 10: D

Using Kepler's Third Law, $T^2 \propto r^3$,

$$\frac{T_1^2}{r_1^3} = \frac{T_2^2}{r_2^3}$$

$$T_2^2 = T_1^2 \left(\frac{r_2}{r_1}\right)^3$$

$$= T_1^2 \left(\frac{1}{4^3}\right)$$

$$T_2 = T_1 \sqrt{\frac{1}{64}}$$

$$= \frac{T_1}{8}$$

$$= \frac{24}{8}$$

$$= \mathbf{3\ hours}$$

Question 11: C

To be $\frac{1}{64}$ of the initial amount, 6 half-lives must have passed since

$$\left(\frac{1}{2}\right)^6 = \frac{1}{64}$$

The total time is therefore $6 \times 3 =$ **18 days**

Question 12: B

The side length of each small cube will be

$$\frac{x}{\sqrt[3]{64}} = \frac{x}{4} \text{ cm}$$

The surface area of each small cube is therefore

$$6 \times \left(\frac{x}{4}\right) \times \left(\frac{x}{4}\right) = \frac{3x^2}{8} \text{ cm}^2$$

Total surface area of all 64 small cubes is therefore

$$64 \times \frac{3x^2}{8} = \mathbf{24x^2 \text{ cm}^2}$$

Question 13

a) On any given throw,

$$P(\text{even}) = P(\text{odd}) = \frac{1}{2}$$

There are three different permutations of two odd rolls and one even roll, so

$$P(2 \text{ odd}, 1 \text{ even}) = 3 \times \frac{1}{2} \times \frac{1}{2} \times \frac{1}{2} = \frac{3}{8}$$

b) This is a binomial distribution, where $n = 3$ and $p = \frac{1}{6}$:

$$P(\text{one } 6) = 3 \times \frac{1}{6} \times \left(\frac{5}{6}\right)^2$$

$$= \frac{25}{72}$$

c) This is equivalent to the probability that at least one 3 is thrown AND no 4, 5 or 6 is thrown. First, calculate the probability that no 4, 5 or 6 is thrown:

$$P(\text{only } 1,2,3) = \left(\frac{1}{2}\right)^3 = \frac{1}{8}$$

All combinations where there is at least one 3 are now valid:

$$P(\text{at least one } 3) = 1 - P(\text{no } 3)$$

$$= 1 - \left(\frac{2}{3}\right)^3 = \frac{19}{27}$$

$$\therefore P(\text{largest number is three}) = \frac{1}{8} \times \frac{19}{27} = \frac{19}{216}$$

Question 14

The height of the arrow above the cliff is given by the equation

$$s \uparrow = ut + \frac{1}{2}at^2$$

where $u = 30 \sin 30 = 15$ ms^{-1} and $a = -g = -10$ ms^{-2}. This gives

$$s \uparrow = 15t - 5t^2$$

When the arrow reaches the sea, its vertical displacement will be -20 m:

$$-20 = 15t - 5t^2$$
$$t^2 - 3t - 4 = 0$$
$$(t - 4)(t + 1) = 0$$

The time must therefore be $t = 4$ s.

The horizontal displacement of the arrow is also given by the formula

$$s \rightarrow = ut + \frac{1}{2}at^2$$

where in this case $u = 30 \cos 30 = 15\sqrt{3}$ ms^{-1} and $a = 0$ as we have assumed no air resistance. The horizontal displacement at $t = 4$ is therefore

$$s \rightarrow = 15\sqrt{3} \times 4$$
$$= 60\sqrt{3} \text{ m}$$

Question 15

This is a geometric progression with first term 1 and common ratio $-e^{-2x}$. The sum to infinity is therefore given by:

$$S_\infty = \frac{a}{1-r}$$

$$= \frac{1}{1-(-e^{-2x})}$$

$$= \frac{1}{1+e^{-2x}}$$

For this to be valid,

$$|r| < 1$$
$$|-e^{-2x}| < 1$$
$$|e^{-2x}| < 1$$

We can therefore see that, for this condition to be satisfied,

$$2x > 0$$
$$\boldsymbol{x > 0}$$

Question 16

a) Use the substitution $u = 1 + \cos x$, so $\frac{du}{dx} = -\sin x$. Substitute these into the integration:

$$\int_0^{\frac{\pi}{2}} \frac{\sin x}{1+\cos x}\,dx = \int_0^{\frac{\pi}{2}} \frac{1}{u}\left(-\frac{du}{dx}\right) dx$$

$$= -\int_{x=0}^{x=\frac{\pi}{2}} \frac{1}{u}\,du$$

$$= -[\ln u]_{x=0}^{x=\frac{\pi}{2}}$$

$$= -[\ln(1+\cos x)]_0^{\frac{\pi}{2}}$$

$$= -[\ln(1) - \ln(2)]$$

$$= \boldsymbol{\ln 2}$$

b) Use the substitution $u = 2x^3 + 8$, so $\frac{du}{dx} = 6x^2$. Substitute these into the integration:

$$\int_0^3 \frac{x^2}{2x^3 + 8}\,dx = \int_0^3 \frac{1}{6}\frac{du}{dx}\left(\frac{1}{u}\right)dx$$

$$= \frac{1}{6}\int_{x=0}^{x=3} \frac{1}{u}\,du$$

$$= \frac{1}{6}\left[\ln u\right]_{x=0}^{x=3}$$

$$= \frac{1}{6}\left[\ln(2x^3 + 8)\right]_0^3$$

$$= \frac{1}{6}(\ln 62 - \ln 8)$$

$$= \frac{1}{6}\ln\left(\frac{31}{4}\right)$$

Question 17

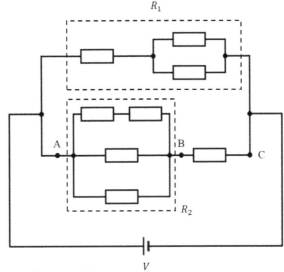

a) The resistance of group R_1 is

$$R_1 = R + \frac{R}{2} = \frac{3R}{2}$$

The resistance of group R_2 is given by

$$\frac{1}{R_2} = \frac{1}{2R} + \frac{1}{R} + \frac{1}{R}$$

$$\frac{1}{R_2} = \frac{5}{2R}$$

$$R_2 = \frac{2R}{5}$$

Hence the resistance of the bottom line is

$$\frac{2R}{5} + R = \frac{7R}{5}$$

The total resistance of the circuit is therefore

$$\frac{1}{R_T} = \frac{2}{3R} + \frac{5}{7R}$$

$$= \frac{29}{21R}$$

$$\boldsymbol{R_T = \frac{21R}{29}}$$

b) The potential difference between A and C is equal to V, and so the potential difference between A and B is given by

$$V_{AB} = \frac{R_2}{R_2 + R} V$$

$$= \frac{2R/5}{7R/5} V$$

$$= \frac{2}{7} V$$

Question 18

A regular hexagon can be divided into six equilateral triangles. The area of each triangle is given by

$$A_{triangle} = \frac{1}{2} ab \sin C$$

$$= \frac{1}{2} \times 5^2 \times \sin 60$$

$$= \frac{25\sqrt{3}}{4} \ m^2$$

The total area of the field is $\frac{75\sqrt{3}}{2} \ m^2$ and so the number of plants is

$$\frac{75\sqrt{3}}{2} \Big/ \frac{\sqrt{3}}{4} = \textbf{150 plants.}$$

Question 19

Volume of sphere $= \frac{4}{3}\pi r^3$.

Volume of cone $= \frac{1}{3}\pi r^2 h$.

$$V_{sphere} = 2V_{cone}$$
$$\frac{4}{3}\pi r^3 = 2\left(\frac{1}{3}\pi r^2 h\right)$$
$$h = 2r$$

The surface area of cone can be calculated as follows:

$$S = \pi r(r + l), \text{ where } l = \sqrt{h^2 + r^2}$$
$$S = \pi r\left(r + \sqrt{4r^2 + r^2}\right)$$
$$= \pi r\left(r + \sqrt{5}r\right)$$
$$= \boldsymbol{\pi r^2(1 + \sqrt{5})}$$

Question 20

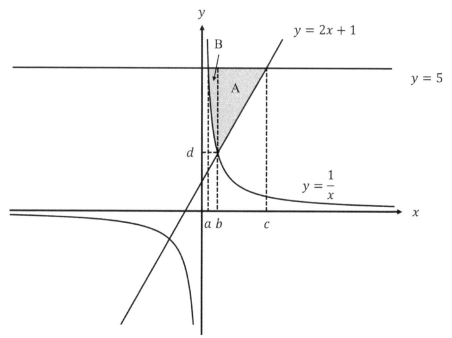

By setting the relevant equations equal to each other, the values of a, b, c and d can be found to be $a = \frac{1}{5}$, $b = \frac{1}{2}$, $c = 2$ and $d = 2$.

From the sketch above, the shaded area can be split into two:
Area A: between $y = 5$ and $y = 2x + 1$
Area B: between $y = 5$ and $y = \frac{1}{x}$

Area A can be found by considering the area of the triangle it represents:

$$A_A = \frac{1}{2} \times \left(2 - \frac{1}{2}\right) \times (5 - 2) = \frac{9}{4}$$

Area B can be found by subtracting the area under $y = \dfrac{1}{x}$ from $5 \times (b - a)$:

$$A_B = 5 \times \left(\frac{1}{2} - \frac{1}{5}\right) - \int_{\frac{1}{5}}^{\frac{1}{2}} \frac{1}{x}\,dx$$

$$= \frac{3}{2} - [\ln x]_{\frac{1}{5}}^{\frac{1}{2}}$$

$$= \frac{3}{2} - \left(\ln\left(\frac{1}{2}\right) - \ln\left(\frac{1}{5}\right)\right)$$

$$= \frac{3}{2} + \ln 2 - \ln 5$$

$$= \frac{3}{2} + \ln\left(\frac{2}{5}\right)$$

The total area is therefore

$$A = A_A + A_B$$

$$= \frac{9}{4} + \frac{3}{2} + \ln\left(\frac{2}{5}\right)$$

$$A = \frac{15}{4} + \ln\left(\frac{2}{5}\right)$$

Question 21

Implicit differentiation of the equation of the circle is required:

$$x^2 + y^2 = 25$$

$$\frac{d}{dx}(x^2) + \frac{d}{dx}(y^2) = \frac{d}{dx}(25)$$

$$2x + 2y\frac{dy}{dx} = 0$$

$$\frac{dy}{dx} = -\frac{x}{y}$$

The gradient of the tangent at (-3, 4) is therefore

$$m = -\frac{(-3)}{4} = \frac{3}{4}$$

The equation of the tangent can then be found:

$$y - y_1 = m(x - x_1)$$

$$y - 4 = \frac{3}{4}(x + 3)$$

$$y = \frac{3}{4}x + \frac{25}{4}$$

Question 22

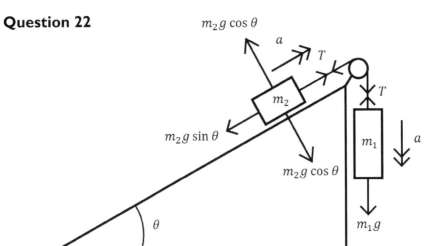

Apply Newton's second law to each mass.

For m_1:

$$m_1 g - T = m_1 a$$
$$T = m_1(g - a) \quad (1)$$

For m_2:

$$T - m_2 g \sin \theta = m_2 a$$
$$T = m_2(a + g \sin \theta) \quad (2)$$

Set (1) equal to (2):

$$m_1(g - a) = m_2(a + g \sin \theta)$$
$$m_2 a + m_1 a = m_1 g - m_2 g \sin \theta$$

$$\boldsymbol{a = \frac{g(m_1 - m_2 \sin \theta)}{(m_1 + m_2)}}$$

Substitute this back into (1):

$$T = m_1 \left(g - \frac{g(m_1 - m_2 \sin \theta)}{(m_1 + m_2)} \right)$$
$$T = m_1 \left(\frac{g(m_1 + m_2) - g(m_1 - m_2 \sin \theta)}{m_1 + m_2} \right)$$
$$\boldsymbol{T = g m_1 m_2 \left(\frac{1 + \sin \theta}{m_1 + m_2} \right)}$$

a) The maximum friction experienced by m_2 when stationary is given by
$$F = \mu_s R$$
$$F = \mu_s m_2 g \cos \theta$$
For m_2 to stay at rest, the acceleration of the whole system must be zero. Hence, for m_1:
$$m_1 g - T = 0$$
$$T = m_1 g \quad (3)$$

For m_2:
$$T - m_2 g \sin \theta - \mu_s(m_2 g \cos \theta) = 0$$
$$T = g m_2(\sin \theta + \mu_s \cos \theta) \quad (4)$$
Set (3) equal to (4):
$$m_1 g = g m_2(\sin \theta + \mu_s \cos \theta)$$
$$\frac{m_1}{m_2} = (\sin \theta + \mu_s \cos \theta)$$

b) For m_2 to accelerate, the static friction coefficient must still be used, as we are considering the situation where the masses are initially at rest. For m_1:
$$m_1 g - T = m_1 a$$
$$T = m_1(g - a) \quad (5)$$
For m_2:
$$T - m_2 g \sin \theta - \mu_s(m_2 g \cos \theta) = m_2 a$$
$$T = m_2(a + g(\sin \theta + \mu_s \cos \theta)) \quad (6)$$
Set (5) equal to (6):
$$m_1(g - a) = m_2(a + g(\sin \theta + \mu_s \cos \theta))$$
$$m_2 a + m_1 a = m_1 g - m_2 g(\sin \theta + \mu_s \cos \theta)$$
$$a = \frac{g(m_1 - m_2(\sin \theta + \mu_s \cos \theta))}{m_1 + m_2}$$
For m_2 to accelerate, $a > 0$:
$$\frac{g(m_1 - m_2(\sin \theta + \mu_s \cos \theta))}{m_1 + m_2} > 0$$
$$\frac{m_1}{m_2} > \sin \theta + \mu_s \cos \theta$$

To derive an expression for the tension, substitute the expression for acceleration back into (5):

$$T = m_1 \left(g - \frac{g\left(m_1 - m_2(\sin\theta + \mu_s \cos\theta)\right)}{(m_1 + m_2)} \right)$$

$$T = m_1 \left(\frac{g(m_1 + m_2) - g\left(m_1 - m_2(\sin\theta + \mu_s \cos\theta)\right)}{m_1 + m_2} \right)$$

$$\boldsymbol{T = gm_1 m_2 \left(\frac{1 + \sin\theta + \mu_s \cos\theta}{m_1 + m_2} \right)}$$

END OF PAPER

Mock Paper C ANSWERS

Question 1: C

The most efficient way to approach this problem is by spotting that

$$(2 - x)^2 = \left(-(x - 2)\right)^2 = (x - 2)^2$$

Therefore,

$$(2 - x)^2(2 + x)^4(x - 2)^2 = (2 - x)^4(2 + x)^4$$
$$= \left((2 - x)(2 + x)\right)^4$$
$$= (2^2 - x^2)^4$$

This shows that all terms must have an even power, and so the coefficient of x^3 is **zero**. Fully expanding the brackets would also give the same answer.

Question 2: A

Use partial fractions:

$$\frac{1}{x^2 + x - 6} = \frac{1}{(x + 3)(x - 2)}$$
$$\frac{1}{(x + 3)(x - 2)} = \frac{A}{(x + 3)} + \frac{B}{(x - 2)}$$
$$\frac{1}{(x + 3)(x - 2)} = \frac{A(x - 2) + B(x + 3)}{(x + 3)(x - 2)}$$
$$A(x - 2) + B(x + 3) = 1$$

Separately considering the x coefficient and constant gives the following simultaneous equations:

$$A + B = 0 \quad (1)$$
$$3B - 2A = 1 \quad (2)$$

Substitute $A = -B$ into (2):

$$3B - 2(-B) = 1$$
$$B = \frac{1}{5}$$

Substitute back into (I):

$$A = -\frac{1}{5}$$

$$\therefore \frac{1}{x^2 + x - 6} = \frac{1}{5}\left(\frac{1}{x - 2} - \frac{1}{x + 3}\right)$$

Hence:

$$\int_3^4 \frac{1}{x^2 + x - 6} dx = \frac{1}{5}\int_3^4 \left(\frac{1}{x - 2} - \frac{1}{x + 3}\right) dx$$

$$= \frac{1}{5}[\ln(x - 2) - \ln(x + 3)]_3^4$$

$$= \frac{1}{5}[(\ln 2 - \ln 7) - (\ln 1 - \ln 6)]$$

$$= \frac{1}{5}(\ln 2 - \ln 7 + \ln 6)$$

$$= \mathbf{0.2\ln\left(\frac{12}{7}\right)}$$

Question 3: A

$$f(x) = e^{-2x} + x^2$$
$$f'(x) = -2e^{-2x} + 2x$$
$$f''(x) = (-2)(-2)e^{-2x} + 2$$
$$= \mathbf{4e^{-2x} + 2}$$

Question 4: D

First, we need to find the gradient of the tangent:

$$\frac{dy}{dx} = 6x$$

$$m = \left.\frac{dy}{dx}\right|_{x=1}$$

$$= 6$$

The equation of the tangent is then given by

$$y - y_1 = m(x - x_1)$$
$$y - 3 = 6(x - 1)$$
$$\therefore \mathbf{y = 6x - 3}$$

Question 5: C

Use the quotient rule:

$$\frac{dy}{dx} = \frac{2(\cos(2x+5))(x^2+6x) - (2x+6)\sin(2x+5)}{(x^2+6x)^2}$$

Question 6: B

This is a geometric series with first term 1 and common ratio $\frac{1}{2}$:

$$S_\infty = \frac{a}{1-r} = \frac{1}{1-\frac{1}{2}} = 2$$

Question 7: D

Use the equation $g = \frac{GM}{r^2}$:

$$\frac{g_{moon}}{g_{earth}} = \frac{M_{moon}/r_{moon}^2}{M_{earth}/r_{earth}^2}$$

$$\frac{g_{moon}}{g_{earth}} = \frac{M_{moon}}{M_{earth}} \times \frac{r_{earth}^2}{r_{moon}^2}$$

Since the masses of the moon and earth are given by the formula

$$M = \frac{4}{3}\rho\pi r^3$$

where ρ is constant,

$$\frac{g_{moon}}{g_{earth}} = \frac{r_{moon}^3}{r_{earth}^3} \times \frac{r_{earth}^2}{r_{moon}^2}$$

$$\frac{g_{moon}}{g_{earth}} = \frac{r_{moon}}{r_{earth}}$$

$$g_{moon} \approx 10 \times \frac{1}{3.5}$$

$$g_{moon} \approx 2.9 \text{ ms}^{-2}$$

Question 8: A

For an ideal gas: $PV = nRT = \dfrac{N}{N_A}RT$.

$$\frac{N}{V} = \frac{PN_A}{RT} = \frac{(10^5)(6.022 \times 10^{23})}{(8.314)(298.15)} \approx 2.4 \times 10^{25} \text{ m}^{-3}$$

This is the number of atoms or molecules per unit volume, hence the volume occupied by each atom is $\dfrac{1}{2.4 \times 10^{25}} \approx 4.2 \times 10^{-26} \text{ m}^3$.

Average separation is therefore $\sqrt[3]{4.2 \times 10^{-26}} \approx \mathbf{3.5 \times 10^{-9}}$ **m**

Question 9: C

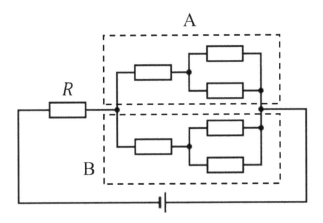

The resistance of network A is given by

$$R_A = R + \frac{R}{2} = \frac{3R}{2}$$

The resistance of network B is equal to that of A, and so the combined resistance of A and B is

$$\frac{1}{R_{AB}} = \frac{2}{3R} + \frac{2}{3R}$$

$$R_{AB} = \frac{3R}{4}$$

The total resistance of the circuit is therefore $R + \dfrac{3R}{4} = \dfrac{7R}{4}$.

Question 10: D

Statement (i) is correct, and statement (ii) is correct as well. Its period is 24 hours (hence (iii) is incorrect), and its movement is in the same direction to earth's rotation (to achieve its stationary status), hence statement (iv) is incorrect as well. As it appears always to be on the same point in the sky, it enables antennas to be pointed at fixed position, hence statement (v) is correct.

Question 11: A

The correct order of visible light is (from shortest to longest wavelength): violet-blue-green-yellow-orange-red.

Question 12: E

Let there initially be x of sample B and $2x$ of sample A. After 36 days, 6 half-lives will have passed for sample A:

$$A_{36} = 2x \times \left(\frac{1}{2}\right)^6$$

$$= \frac{x}{32}$$

Similarly, 4 half-lives will have passed for sample B:

$$B_{36} = x \times \left(\frac{1}{2}\right)^4$$

$$= \frac{x}{16}$$

Hence,

$$A_{36} : B_{36} = \frac{x}{32} : \frac{x}{16}$$

$$= 1:2$$

Question 13

First, we need to evaluate the geometric series inside the integral, which has first term 1 and common ratio q:

$$S_{N+1} = \frac{a(1 - r^{N+1})}{1 - r} = \frac{1 - q^{N+1}}{1 - q}$$

Since N is large and $0 \leq q < 1$,

$$q^{N+1} \to 0$$

$$\frac{1 - q^{N+1}}{1 - q} = \frac{1}{1 - q}$$

$$\int_0^{0.5} (1 + q + q^2 + \cdots + q^N)\, dq = \int_0^{0.5} \frac{1}{1 - q}\, dq$$

$$= |-\ln(1 - q)|_0^{0.5}$$

$$= -\ln(0.5) + \ln(1)$$

$$= \ln 2$$

Question 14

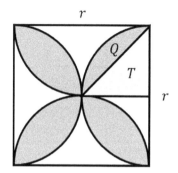

The area of the triangle T above is
$$A_T = \frac{1}{2} \times \frac{r}{2} \times \frac{r}{2} = \frac{r^2}{8}$$

The area of a quarter of a circle $(Q + T)$ is
$$A_{QT} = \frac{1}{4}\pi \left(\frac{r}{2}\right)^2 = \frac{\pi r^2}{16}$$

The area of Q is therefore
$$A_Q = A_{QT} - A_T$$
$$= \frac{\pi r^2}{16} - \frac{r^2}{8}$$
$$= \frac{r^2}{16}(\pi - 2)$$

The total shaded area is then given by
$$A = 8 \times A_Q$$
$$= \frac{r^2}{2}(\pi - 2)$$

Question 15

The angular speed of the club is $\omega = \frac{2\pi}{T} = 20\pi$ rad/s. The speed at which the club hits the ball is therefore $v = r\omega = 20\pi$ ms^{-1}.

The distance that the ball travels is maximised when the golfer hits the ball at an angle of $45°$ to the horizontal.

The time that the ball is in the air is twice the time that it takes to reach maximum height, since the motion of the ball is parabolic:

$$v \uparrow = u + at$$
$$0 = 20\pi \sin 45 - gt_{maxheight}$$
$$t_{maxheight} = \frac{10\sqrt{2}\pi}{g}$$

Since this is half the time the ball takes to reach its maximum distance,

$$t_{max} = \frac{20\sqrt{2}\pi}{g}$$

The horizontal distance travelled by the ball is given by

$$s \rightarrow = 20\pi t \cos 45$$

So the maximum distance the golfer could hit the ball is

$$20\pi \cos 45 \times \frac{20\sqrt{2}\pi}{g} = \frac{400\pi^2}{g} \approx \mathbf{400\ m}$$

Question 16

Since energy is conserved, all kinetic energy must come from elastic potential energy. Hence:

$$\frac{1}{2}mv^2 = \frac{1}{2}kx^2$$
$$k = \frac{mv^2}{x^2}$$
$$= \frac{(0.05)(15)^2}{(0.1)^2}$$
$$= \mathbf{1125\ Nm^{-1}}$$

This limit would be unchanged on the moon as it is not dependent on gravitational acceleration.

Question 17

Let there be x green flowers. There will then be $2x$ yellow, $6x$ red, $24x$ blue and $120x$ purple. The total number of flowers is therefore $153x$.

a) $P(\text{yellow}) = \dfrac{2}{153}$

b) $P(\text{red}) = \dfrac{6}{153} = \dfrac{2}{51}$

c) $P(\text{purple}) = \dfrac{120}{153} = \dfrac{40}{51}$

Question 18

The total surface area of the planetarium to be painted is equal to the area of the cylinder shell plus the area of the hemisphere.

Area of wall $= 2\pi R h$

Area of hemisphere $= 2\pi R^2$

The volume of paint needed is given by total area × thickness:

$$V = (2\pi R h + 2\pi R^2) \times t$$
$$= 2\pi R(h + R)t$$

Question 19

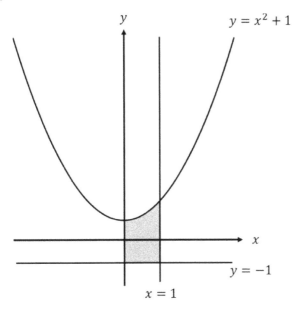

The total shaded area is equal to the rectangle under the x-axis plus the area between the curve $y = x^2 + 1$ and the x-axis. Therefore the total area is

$$A = 1 + \int_0^1 (x^2 + 1)\, dx$$

$$= 1 + \left[\frac{x^3}{3} + x\right]_0^1$$

$$= 1 + \frac{1}{3} + 1$$

$$= \frac{7}{3}$$

Question 20

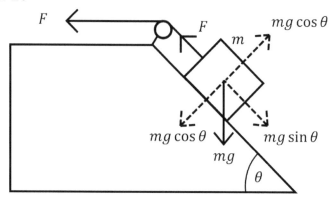

a) When the block is at rest, resolving forces parallel to the slope gives
$$F = \mu_s R + mg \sin \theta$$
$$= mg(\mu_s \cos \theta + \sin \theta)$$

b) When the block is moving at constant velocity, the forces will again be balanced but the static friction coefficient will now be replaced by the kinetic friction coefficient, μ_k.
$$F = mg(\mu_k \cos \theta + \sin \theta)$$

Question 21

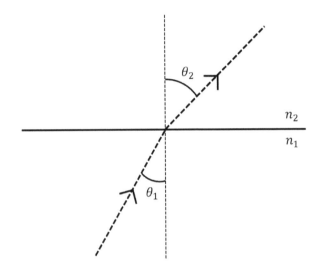

Snell's law:
$$n_1 \sin \theta_1 = n_2 \sin \theta_2$$
When the angle of incidence reaches a certain critical value, the refracted ray lies along the boundary and so the angle of refraction is 90°.
$$n_1 \sin \theta_c = n_2 \sin 90$$
$$\sin \theta_c = \frac{n_2}{n_1}$$

When the light is incident on the liquid-glass surface, the critical angle is given by
$$\sin \theta_c = \frac{n_{glass}}{n_{liquid}}$$
$$= \frac{1.52}{1.63}$$
$$= 0.93$$
$$\theta_c \approx 69°$$

END OF PAPER

Mock Paper D ANSWERS

Question 1: C

Factorising the equation gives
$$x^3 - 7x + 6 = (x^2 + x - 6)(x - 1)$$
$$= (x + 3)(x - 2)(x - 1) = 0$$
The roots are therefore $x = -3, 2, 1.$

Question 2: B
$$f'(x) = -2\sin x + 2x$$

Question 3: A

Gravitational acceleration is given by the equation $g = \frac{GM}{r^2}$. Since $w = mg$ and mass remains constant,

$$\frac{w_{top}}{w_{ground}} = \frac{g_{top}}{g_{ground}}$$
$$= \frac{1/r_{top}^2}{1/r_{ground}^2}$$
$$= \frac{1/7371^2}{1/6371^2}$$
$$= \frac{6371^2}{7371^2}$$

Question 4: C

The effective spring constant of two springs in parallel is equal to $2k$. Maximum elastic energy occurs when the spring are at their maximum extension:

$$EPE_{max} = \frac{1}{2}(2k)L^2 = kL^2$$

Since energy is conserved, maximum kinetic energy = maximum elastic potential energy.

$$KE_{max} = kL^2$$
$$\frac{1}{2}mv_{max}^2 = kL^2$$
$$v_{max}^2 = \frac{2kL^2}{m}$$
$$v_{max} = \sqrt{\frac{2k}{m}}L$$

Question 5: B

For an ideal gas,

$$pV = nRT$$

In this case pressure, moles and R are constant. Hence:

$$\frac{V}{T} = \frac{nR}{p} = constant$$
$$\frac{V_1}{T_1} = \frac{V_2}{T_2}$$
$$\frac{T_2}{T_1} = \frac{V_2}{V_1}$$
$$T_2 = \frac{1}{2}T_1$$

Question 6: E

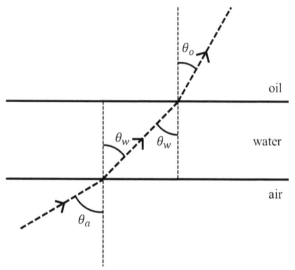

Snell's law states that

$$n_a \sin \theta_a = n_w \sin \theta_w = n_o \sin \theta_o$$
$$n_a \sin \theta_a = n_o \sin \theta_o$$

Since $n_a = 1$ and the question states that $\theta_a = 60°$ and $n_o = 1.55$,

$$\sin 60 = 1.55 \sin \theta_o$$
$$\theta_o = \sin^{-1} \left(\frac{\sin 60}{1.55} \right)$$
$$= \sin^{-1}(0.559)$$
$$= \mathbf{34.0°}$$

Question 7: A

First, differentiate to find the gradient of the tangent:

$$y = (8x - 4x^2)^{\frac{1}{2}}$$

$$\frac{dy}{dx} = \frac{1}{2}(8x - 4x^2)^{-\frac{1}{2}}(8 - 8x)$$

$$= \frac{8 - 8x}{2\sqrt{8x - 4x^2}}$$

$$m = \frac{dy}{dx}\Big|_{x=2}$$

$$= \frac{8 - 8(2)}{2\sqrt{8(2) - 4(2)^2}}$$

$$= -\frac{8}{2\sqrt{0}} \rightarrow -\infty$$

From this, we therefore know that the tangent must be a straight vertical line. Hence, the equation of the tangent is $x = 2$.

Question 8: D

Using these roots, the corresponding factors can be multiplied to give the equation:

$$f(x) = (x + 1)(x)(x - 1)$$

$$= x(x^2 - 1)$$

$$= x^3 - x$$

Question 9: A

The area is shown in the sketch below:

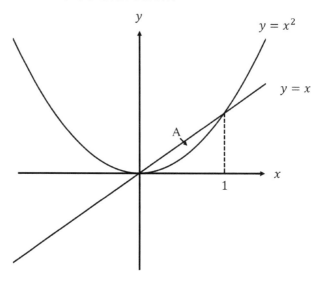

The area A is equal to the area under the line $y = x$ minus the area under the curve $y = x^2$.

$$A = \int_0^1 x \, dx - \int_0^1 x^2 \, dx$$

$$= \int_0^1 (x - x^2) \, dx$$

$$= \left[\frac{x^2}{2} - \frac{x^3}{3} \right]_0^1$$

$$= \frac{1}{2} - \frac{1}{3}$$

$$= \frac{1}{6}$$

Question 10: B

Use the equation for gravitational acceleration:

$$g = \frac{GM}{r^2}$$

Since G and M are constant in both cases,

$$\frac{g_2}{g_1} = \frac{r_1^2}{r_2^2}$$

$$g_2 \approx 10 \times \left(\frac{1}{2}\right)^2$$

$$g_2 \approx 2.5 \text{ ms}^{-2}$$

Question 11: E

Statement (i) is correct; statement (ii) is incorrect as gamma rays have the shortest wavelengths; statement (iii) is correct; statement (iv) is correct as the wavelength would be $\lambda = \frac{c}{f} = \frac{3 \times 10^8}{10^9} = 0.3$ m; statement (v) is incorrect (red has lowest frequency and violet has highest frequency).

Question 12: D

As momentum is conserved, then:

$$m_{bullet} v_{bullet} = (m_{ball} + m_{bullet}) v_{final}$$

$$v_{final} = \frac{m_{bullet} v_{bullet}}{m_{ball} + m_{bullet}}$$

$$v_{final} = \frac{0.1 \times 100}{(2 + 0.1)} = \frac{10}{2.1} \approx 4.8 \text{ ms}^{-1}$$

Question 13

a) Use the $\sin 2x$ identity:

$$\int_{-\frac{\pi}{2}}^{\frac{\pi}{2}} \sin x \cos x \, dx = \frac{1}{2} \int_{-\frac{\pi}{2}}^{\frac{\pi}{2}} \sin 2x \, dx$$

$\sin 2x$ is an odd function and so has an equal and opposite area on either side of the y-axis. Since integration gives the area under a curve, these two areas will cancel each other out in the integral, giving **0**.

b)

$$\int \left(x^2 e^{x^3} + \sin^2 x\right) dx = \int x^2 e^{x^3} \, dx + \int \sin^2 x \, dx$$

The first integral can be solved using substitution. Let $u = x^3$; $\frac{du}{dx} = 3x^2$:

$$\int x^2 e^{x^3} \, dx = \int \frac{1}{3} \frac{du}{dx} e^u \, dx$$

$$= \frac{1}{3} \int e^u \, du$$

$$= \frac{1}{3} e^{x^3} + c$$

The second integral can be solved by using the $\cos 2x$ identity:

$$\cos 2x = \cos^2 x - \sin^2 x$$
$$= 1 - 2\sin^2 x$$
$$\sin^2 x = \frac{1}{2}(1 - \cos 2x)$$

Substitute this in to the second integral and the integration can then be performed:

$$\int \sin^2 x \, dx = \int \frac{1}{2}(1 - \cos 2x) \, dx$$

$$= \frac{x}{2} - \frac{\sin 2x}{4} + c$$

$$\therefore \int \left(x^2 e^{x^3} + \sin^2 x\right) dx = \frac{1}{3} e^{x^3} + \frac{x}{2} - \frac{\sin 2x}{4} + c$$

Question 14

The volume of snow available is $20 \times 20 \times 0.05 = 20 \text{ m}^3$. The total volume of the snowman is

$$\frac{4}{3}\pi R^3 + \frac{4}{3}\pi(1.5R)^3 + \frac{4}{3}\pi(2R)^3 = \frac{4}{3}\pi\left(\frac{99}{8}R^3\right) = \frac{33\pi R^3}{2}$$

$$\therefore \frac{33}{2}\pi R^3 = 20$$

$$R^3 = \frac{40}{33\pi}$$

$$\therefore R = \sqrt[3]{\frac{40}{33\pi}} \text{ m}$$

Question 15

Expressions for the number of green and red apples and green pears are given in the question. The number of red pears can also be calculated as $2(x - 3)$. The total number of apples is therefore

$$(2x - 1) + (x + 2) + (x - 3) + 2(x - 3) = 6x - 8$$

a) $P(\text{apple}) = \dfrac{2x - 1 + x + 2}{6x - 8} = \dfrac{3x + 1}{6x - 8}$

b) $P(\text{green}) = \dfrac{2x - 1 + x - 3}{6x - 8} = \dfrac{3x - 4}{6x - 8} = \dfrac{1}{2}$

c) $P(\text{red pear}) = \dfrac{2(x - 3)}{6x - 8} = \dfrac{x - 3}{3x - 4}$

Question 16

Area of largest circle:

$$L = \pi(4)^2 = 16\pi$$

Combined area of smaller circles:

$$S = \pi\left(\frac{5}{2}\right)^2 + \pi\left(\frac{3}{2}\right)^2 = \frac{34}{4}\pi = \frac{17}{2}\pi$$

Area of shaded region:

$$\frac{1}{2}(L - S) = \frac{1}{2}\left(16\pi - \frac{17}{2}\pi\right) = \frac{15}{4}\pi$$

Question 17

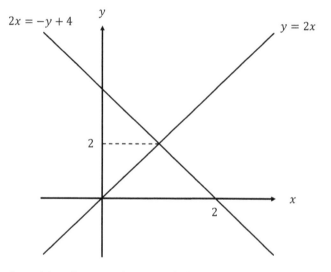

The area enclosed by the two lines and the x-axis is a triangle with height 2 and base 2. The area of the triangle is therefore

$$A = \frac{1}{2} \times b \times h$$

$$= \frac{1}{2} \times 2 \times 2 = 2$$

Question 18

Consider the system over the top pulley with tension T_1, taking clockwise movement as positive:

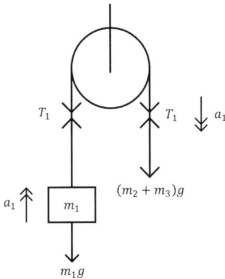

$$(m_2 + m_3)g - m_1g = (m_1 + m_2 + m_3)a_1$$
$$a_1 = \frac{g(m_2 + m_3 - m_1)}{m_1 + m_2 + m_3}$$

The acceleration of the bottom pulley itself must therefore be equal to a_1 (downwards).

Now consider the movement of the string T_2 relative to the bottom pulley (treating the bottom pulley itself as stationary):

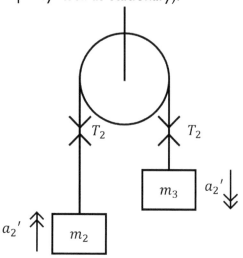

$$m_3 g - m_2 g = (m_2 + m_3)a_2'$$
$$a_2' = \frac{g(m_3 - m_2)}{m_2 + m_3}$$

Including the downwards acceleration of the bottom pulley, the absolute acceleration of m_2 is

$$a_2 = a_2' - a_1$$
$$= \frac{g(m_3 - m_2)}{m_2 + m_3} - \frac{g(m_2 + m_3 - m_1)}{m_1 + m_2 + m_3}$$

Similarly,

$$a_3 = a_2' + a_1$$
$$= \frac{g(m_3 - m_2)}{m_2 + m_3} + \frac{g(m_2 + m_3 - m_1)}{m_1 + m_2 + m_3}$$

Question 19

The time the ball spends in the air is equal to twice the time it takes for the ball to reach maximum height, as its motion is parabolic. Since the vertical component of initial speed is $u \sin(30) = \frac{u}{2}$,

$$0 = \frac{u}{2} - g\frac{t_{max}}{2}$$

$$t_{max} = \frac{u}{g}$$

Horizontally, there is no acceleration and the initial horizontal velocity is $u \cos 30 = \frac{\sqrt{3}}{2}u$:

$$\frac{\sqrt{3}}{2}u \times t_{max} = 100$$

$$\frac{\sqrt{3}}{2}\frac{u^2}{g} = 100$$

$$u = \left(\frac{200g}{\sqrt{3}}\right)^{\frac{1}{2}}$$

The range can be improved by increasing the angle of launch to 45° (the optimal angle for launching a projectile).

Question 20

The energy required to move the cable car and passengers from point A to point B = change in gravitational energy + energy dissipated due to friction.

The total energy input required is given by E_{tot} = energy required / efficiency of the motor.

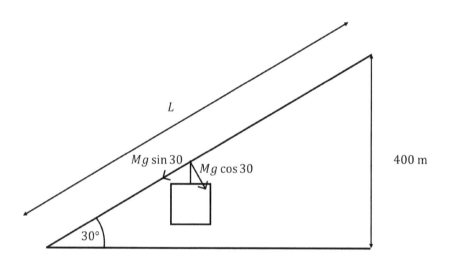

The change in gravitational energy is given by
$$\Delta GPE = Mg\Delta h$$
$$= (200 + 300) \times 10 \times 400$$
$$= 2,000,000 \text{ J}$$

The length of the cable is given by $L = \dfrac{\Delta h}{\sin(30)} = 800$ m.

Energy dissipated due to friction = frictional force × distance

$$= \mu M g \cos 30 \times L$$

$$= 0.02 \times (200 + 300) \times 10 \times \frac{\sqrt{3}}{2} \times 800$$

$$= 40000\sqrt{3} \text{ J}$$

$$E_{tot} = \frac{40000\sqrt{3} + 2000000}{0.1}$$

$$= \mathbf{400000\left(\sqrt{3} + 50\right) J}$$

$$P = \frac{E_{tot}}{t}$$

$$= \frac{400000\left(\sqrt{3} + 50\right)}{120}$$

$$= \frac{\mathbf{10000\left(\sqrt{3} + 50\right)}}{3} \text{ W}$$

Question 21

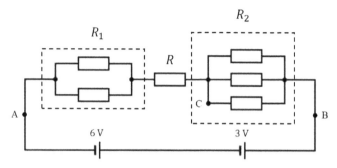

Using the laws for parallel resistors, R_1 and R_2 can be determined to be

$$R_1 = \frac{R}{2} \text{ and } R_2 = \frac{R}{3}$$

a) Between A and B, the voltage will be equal to the sum of the batteries' emf:

$$V_{AB} = 9 \text{ V}$$

b) Between A and C, the potential divider equation is required:

$$V_{AC} = 9 \times \frac{R_1 + R}{R_1 + R + R_2}$$

$$= 9 \times \frac{R/2 + R}{R/2 + R + R/3}$$

$$= 9 \times \frac{3/2}{11/6}$$

$$= \frac{81}{11} \text{ V}$$

Question 22

In an equilateral triangle, the distance to the centre from each vertex is

$$R = \frac{\sqrt{3}a}{3}$$

The electric field produced by each charge is given by

$$E = \frac{k(\pm q)}{R^2}$$

Consider the configuration of the charges as shown in the diagram below.

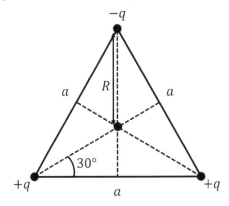

The electric field produced by the charge $-q$ only has a vertical component at the centre, whereas the field from the two positive charges will have both vertical and horizontal components. The horizontal components, however, will cancel each other out.

At the centre there is only a vertical electric field, the strength of which is given by summing the vertical components of the three fields at this point:

$$|E| = \frac{kq}{\left(\sqrt{3}a/3\right)^2}[2\sin(30) - (-1)] = \frac{6kq}{a^2}$$

Note that the charges are not necessarily in this configuration. The general solution is therefore that the electric field will have magnitude $|E|$ (as above) and direction towards $-q$.

If all the charges had the same sign, **the electric field at the centre would be zero** because the two terms in the brackets in the expression above would cancel each other out (i.e. $2\sin 30 - 1 = 0$).

END OF PAPER

Mock Paper E ANSWERS

Question 1: C

Let $u = x^2 - x - 1$, then $\frac{du}{dx} = 2x - 1$. Substitute this into the integral:

$$\int_3^4 \frac{2x - 1}{x^2 - x - 1} dx = \int_3^4 \frac{1}{u}\left(\frac{du}{dx}\right) dx$$

$$= \int_{x=3}^{x=4} \frac{1}{u} du$$

$$= [\ln u]_{x=3}^{x=4}$$

$$= [\ln(x^2 - x - 1)]_3^4$$

$$= \ln 11 - \ln 5$$

$$= \ln\left(\frac{11}{5}\right)$$

Question 2: A

Let $u = x^2$, then $\frac{du}{dx} = 2x$ and $f(x) = \ln^2 u$.

Applying the chain rules then gives

$$\frac{df(x)}{dx} = \frac{df(x)}{du}\frac{du}{dx}$$

$$= \left[2\ln(u)\left(\frac{1}{u}\right)\right](2x)$$

$$= 2\ln(x^2)\left(\frac{1}{x^2}\right)(2x)$$

$$= \frac{4\ln(x^2)}{x}$$

Question 3: E

$$\sum_{i=0}^{\infty} 5r^i = 5 + 5r + 5r^2 + \cdots$$

This is therefore a geometric progression with first term 5 and common ratio r. Hence:

$$\sum_{i=0}^{\infty} 5r^i = \frac{a}{1-r} = 10$$

$$\frac{5}{1-r} = 10$$

$$\therefore r = 1 - \frac{1}{2} = \frac{1}{2}$$

Question 4: B

$$\log_2 \frac{x}{y} = 3$$

$$\frac{x}{y} = 2^3 = 8 \quad (1)$$

$$6y + x = 14 \quad (2)$$

Substitute (1) into (2):

$$6y + (8y) = 14$$

$$y = 1 \rightarrow x = 8$$

Question 5: A

The possible prime numbers are 2, 3, 5 and 7. There are two red suits: hearts and diamonds. Hence, the total number of cards that are both prime and red are 8 (out of 52). The probability is therefore

$$\frac{8}{52} = \frac{2}{13}$$

Question 6: D

As all of the options are quadratic functions, take the general formula for a quadratic function in completed square form:

$$y = a(x - b)^2 + c$$

The minimum of this function must be at (b, c), which in this case is $(3, -6)$. Therefore

$$y = a(x - 3)^2 - 6$$

To find a, consider the y-intercept:

$$\text{At } x = 0, y = 12$$
$$a(0 - 3)^2 - 6 = 12$$
$$9a - 6 = 12$$
$$a = 2$$

Hence the function is

$$y = 2(x - 3)^2 - 6 = \mathbf{2x^2 - 12x + 12}$$

Question 7: B

Combining the formulae $g = \frac{GM}{r^2}$ and $M = \rho V$ gives

$$g = \frac{G\rho V}{r^2}$$

In this case, g is therefore directly proportional to ρ. Hence, if the density was twice as large, the gravitational acceleration would be double its current value:

$$2 \times 9.81 = \mathbf{19.6 \ ms^{-2}}$$

Question 8: B

As the gas is ideal,

$$PV = nRT$$

$$P = \frac{nRT}{V} = \frac{\left(\frac{m}{M}\right)RT}{a^3}$$

The total force exerted by the gas on the cube is given by

$$F = P \times area$$

$$= \frac{\left(\frac{m}{M}\right)RT}{a^3} \times 6a^2$$

$$= \frac{6\left(\frac{m}{M}\right)RT}{a}$$

Question 9: D

The equation for the emf of a battery with internal resistance R_{int} is

$$V = I(R + R_{int})$$

$$R = \frac{V}{I} - R_{int}$$

$$= \frac{1.5}{0.5} - 0.1 = 2.9 \ \Omega$$

Question 10: A

Kepler's Third Law states that $T^2 \propto r^3$, where T is the orbital period and r is the orbital radius:

$$\frac{T_A^2}{r_A^3} = \frac{T_B^2}{r_B^3}$$

$$T_B^2 = T_A^2 \left(\frac{r_B}{r_A}\right)^3$$

$$= (1000)^2 \left(\frac{8}{2}\right)^3$$

$$= 64 \times 10^6$$

$$\therefore T_B = \sqrt{64 \times 10^6}$$

$$= 8000 \ days$$

Question 11: E

The charge accumulated by the capacitor is

$$q = CV$$
$$= 30 \times 10^{-9} \times 1.5$$
$$= 4.5 \times 10^{-8} \text{ C}$$

Since current is the rate of flow of charge, for constant current:

$$I = \frac{q}{t}$$
$$t = \frac{q}{I}$$
$$= \frac{4.5 \times 10^{-8}}{2 \times 10^{-6}}$$
$$= 2.25 \times 10^{-2} \text{ s} = \textbf{22.5 ms}$$

Question 12: A

Neglecting air resistance, conservation of energy shows that the loss of kinetic energy must be equal to the energy dissipated due to braking.

$$\frac{1}{2}mv^2 = Fd$$
$$F = \frac{mv^2}{2d}$$

Since 72 km/h $= \frac{72 \times 10^3}{3600} = 20 \text{ ms}^{-1}$,

$$F = \frac{100 \times 20^2}{2 \times 100}$$
$$= \textbf{200 N}$$

Question 13

The depth of the pool along one shorter side is 1.5 m, and its depth along the opposite side is

$$1.5 + \tan(3) \times 50 \approx 4 \text{ m}$$

Since the pool has the cross-section of a trapezium, its volume is given by

$$V = \frac{1}{2}(1.5 + 4) \times 20 \times 50$$
$$= 2750 \text{ m}^3$$

The volume of water evaporating per week is

$$20 \times 50 \times 0.001 \times 24 \times 7 = 168 \text{ m}^3$$

The total volume of water required is therefore $2750 + 168 =$ **2918 m^3**

Question 14

Let x be the number of salmon, then there are $3x$ trout and $6x$ cod, giving $10x$ fish in total. The probability of each type of fish being lighter than 2kg is $\frac{1}{4}$ for salmon, $\frac{1}{3}$ for trout and $\frac{1}{2}$ for cod.

a) $P(T > 2 \text{ kg}) = \dfrac{3x}{10x} \times \dfrac{2}{3} = \dfrac{1}{5}$

b) $P(S < 2 \text{ kg}) = \dfrac{x}{10x} \times \dfrac{1}{4} = \dfrac{1}{40}$

c) $P(any > 2 \text{ kg}) = \dfrac{1}{2} \times \dfrac{6x}{10x} + \dfrac{2}{3} \times \dfrac{3x}{10x} + \dfrac{3}{4} \times \dfrac{x}{10x} = \dfrac{23}{40}$

Question 15

Break the shape up into the sections shown in the diagram below:

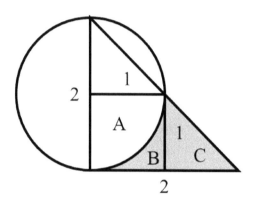

Area A is a quarter of the circle:

$$A_A = \frac{1}{4} \times \pi \times 1^2$$
$$= \frac{\pi}{4}$$

Since A+B is a square of area one,

$$A_B = A_{AB} - A_A$$
$$= 1 - \frac{\pi}{4}$$

Area C is a triangle:

$$A_C = \frac{1}{2} \times 1 \times 1$$
$$= \frac{1}{2}$$

The area of the shaded region is therefore

$$A = A_B + A_C$$
$$= 1 - \frac{\pi}{4} + \frac{1}{2}$$
$$= \frac{3}{2} - \frac{\pi}{4}$$

Question 16

a) Use a substitution for the term inside the sin function. Let $u = 2x - e^{-2x}$, then $\frac{du}{dx} = 2 + 2e^{-2x}$. Substitute this into the integral:

$$\int (1 + e^{-2x}) \sin(2x - e^{-2x}) \, dx = \int \frac{1}{2} \left(\frac{du}{dx}\right) \sin u \, dx$$

$$= \frac{1}{2} \int \sin u \, du$$

$$= -\frac{1}{2} \cos u + c$$

$$= -\frac{1}{2} \cos(2x - e^{-2x}) + c$$

b) First factorise the denominator:
$$(x - 3)(x^2 - 3x + 2) = (x - 3)(x - 2)(x - 1)$$

Then use partial fractions to separate the factors:

$$\frac{3x - 5}{(x - 3)(x - 2)(x - 1)} = \frac{a}{x - 3} + \frac{b}{x - 2} + \frac{c}{x - 1}$$

$$= \frac{a(x - 2)(x - 1) + b(x - 3)(x - 1) + c(x - 3)(x - 2)}{(x - 3)(x - 2)(x - 1)}$$

$$= \frac{(a + b + c)x^2 - (3a + 4b + 5c)x + (2a + 3b + 6c)}{(x - 3)(x - 2)(x - 1)}$$

Consider the coefficients of x^2, x and the constant:
$$a + b + c = 0$$
$$c = -(a + b) \quad (1)$$
$$3a + 4b + 5c = -3 \quad (2)$$
$$2a + 3b + 6c = -5 \quad (3)$$

Substitute (1) into (2) and (3):
$$3a + 4b - 5(a + b) = -3$$
$$2a + b = 3 \quad (4)$$
$$2a + 3b - 6(a + b) = -5$$
$$4a + 3b = 5 \quad (5)$$
$$(5) - 2 \times (4):$$
$$b = -1$$

Substituting back into (4) then (1) gives
$$a = 2 \text{ and } c = -1$$
Hence:
$$\int \frac{3x - 5}{(x - 3)(x - 2)(x - 1)}\, dx = \int \left(\frac{2}{x - 3} - \frac{1}{x - 2} - \frac{1}{x - 1} \right) dx$$
$$= 2\ln(x - 3) - \ln(x - 2) - \ln(x - 1) + c$$

Question 17

To transform from polar coordinates to Cartesian coordinates use the equations $y = r \sin \theta$ and $x = r \cos \theta$. Substitute these into the equation in the question:
$$r^2 \cos^2 \theta - 2r \cos \theta + r^2 \sin^2 \theta = 24$$
$$x^2 - 2x + y^2 = 24$$
$$(x - 1)^2 - 1 + y^2 = 24$$
$$(x - 1)^2 + y^2 = 25$$

This is therefore a circle with centre (1, 0) and radius 5:

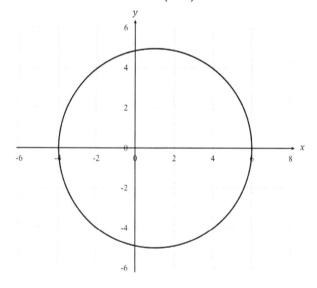

Question 18

As the springs are connected in series, the overall spring constant is given by

$$\frac{1}{k} = \frac{1}{k_1} + \frac{1}{k_2}$$

$$k = \frac{k_1 + k_2}{k_1 k_2}$$

The force in each spring must be the same:

$$F = k_1 l_1 = k_2 l_2$$

$$l_1 = \frac{k_2 l_2}{k_1}$$

The question states that $k_2 < k_1$, so $l_1 < l_2$. This means that when $l_2 = l$ (it is at its maximum extension), $l_1 = \frac{k_2 l}{k_1}$ $(< l)$.

Now consider the conservation of energy to obtain the maximum speed of the ball:

$$KE_{max} = EPE_{max}$$

$$\frac{1}{2} m v_{max}^2 = \frac{1}{2} k_1 l_{1,max}^2 + \frac{1}{2} k_2 l_{2,max}^2$$

$$m v_{max}^2 = k_1 \left(\frac{k_2 l}{k_1}\right)^2 + k_2 l^2$$

$$m v_{max}^2 = l^2 \left(\frac{k_2^2}{k_1} + k_2\right)$$

$$v_{max} = l \left(\frac{k_2}{m} \left(\frac{k_2}{k_1} + 1\right)\right)^{\frac{1}{2}}$$

Question 19

Use the equation for a transformer:

$$\frac{V_S}{V_P} = \frac{N_S}{N_P}$$

$$V_2 = \frac{N_2}{N_1} V$$

The circuit is then effectively the same as the one below:

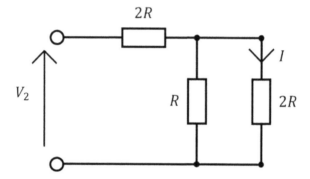

Let the voltage across the two parallel resistors be equal to V_3. These resistors have an effective overall resistance given by

$$\frac{1}{R_{eff}} = \frac{1}{R} + \frac{1}{2R}$$

$$R_{eff} = \frac{2R}{3}$$

The voltage V_3 can then be calculated using the potential divider equation:

$$V_3 = V_2 \times \frac{2R/3}{2R/3 + 2R}$$

$$= \frac{N_2 V}{4N_1}$$

The current is therefore

$$I = \frac{N_2 V}{4N_1} \times \frac{1}{2R}$$

$$= \frac{N_2 V}{8RN_1}$$

Question 20

The total charge inside the sphere at a given radius $(r < R)$ is:

$$q(r < R) = \int_0^r 4\pi r^2 \rho \, dr = \int_0^r 4\pi r^3 a \, dr = a\pi r^4$$

Electric potential is given by

$$E = \frac{kQ}{r^2}$$

The electric potential inside the sphere is therefore

$$E(r < R) = \frac{ka\pi r^4}{r^2} = ka\pi r^2$$

The total charge in the sphere is $Q = a\pi R^4$. Therefore, the electric field outside the sphere is:

$$E(r > R) = \frac{ka\pi R^4}{r^2}$$

Question 21

Since the initial velocity of the rocket is equal to the wind velocity,

$$u_x = w \cos \alpha \text{ and } u_y = w \sin \alpha$$

The height of the rocket is therefore given by

$$h = ut + \frac{1}{2}at^2$$

$$= wt \sin \alpha + \frac{1}{2}(2g - g)t^2$$

$$= wt \sin \alpha + \frac{gt^2}{2}$$

When the rocket reaches a height H,

$$H = wt \sin \alpha + \frac{gt^2}{2}$$

$$gt^2 + 2wt \sin \alpha - 2H = 0$$

Solve the quadratic equation for t:

$$t = \frac{-2w \sin \alpha \pm \sqrt{(2w \sin \alpha)^2 - 4g(-2H)}}{2g}$$

$$t = \frac{-2w \sin \alpha \pm \sqrt{4w^2 \sin^2 \alpha + 8gH}}{2g}$$

$$t = \frac{-w \sin \alpha \pm \sqrt{w^2 \sin^2 \alpha + 2gH}}{g}$$

Since $t > 0$, only the positive solution is possible:

$$t = \frac{-w \sin \alpha + \sqrt{w^2 \sin^2 \alpha + 2gH}}{g}$$

Using this value of t, the horizontal distance travelled by the rocket is therefore

$$D = w \cos \alpha \times t$$

$$\boldsymbol{D = \frac{w \cos \alpha}{g}\left(-w \sin \alpha + \sqrt{w^2 \sin^2 \alpha + 2gH}\right)}$$

Question 22

Consider the following free body diagrams of the masses m_1 and m_2:

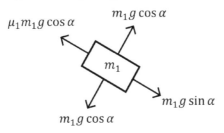

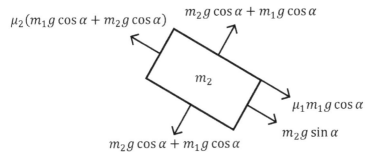

As shown, mass m_2 experiences an extra force of $m_1 g \cos \alpha$ perpendicular to the slope due to the reaction force it exerts on m_1. It also experiences an extra force of $\mu_1 m_1 g \cos \alpha$ parallel to the slope due to the frictional force it exerts on m_1.

a) Resolve forces on m_2 parallel to the slope and use Newton's second law:

$$m_2 a_2 = m_2 g \sin \alpha + \mu_1 m_1 g \cos \alpha - \mu_2 (m_1 g \cos \alpha + m_2 g \cos \alpha)$$

$$a_2 = \frac{g}{m_2} [m_2 \sin \alpha + \mu_1 m_1 \cos \alpha - \mu_2 (m_1 + m_2) \cos \alpha]$$

b) Resolve forces on m_1 parallel to the slope and use Newton's second law:

$$m_1 a_1 = m_1 g \sin \alpha - \mu_1 m_1 g \cos \alpha$$
$$a_1 = g[\sin \alpha - \mu_1 \cos \alpha]$$

c)
$$a_1' = a_1 - a_2$$
$$= g[\sin \alpha - \mu_1 \cos \alpha]$$
$$- \frac{g}{m_2}[m_2 \sin \alpha + \mu_1 m_1 \cos \alpha - \mu_2(m_1 + m_2) \cos \alpha]$$
$$= g\left[\sin \alpha - \mu_1 \cos \alpha - \sin \alpha - \frac{\mu_1 m_1}{m_2}\cos \alpha + \frac{\mu_2 m_1}{m_2}\cos \alpha + \mu_2 \cos \alpha\right]$$
$$= g \cos \alpha\left[-\mu_1 - \frac{\mu_1 m_1}{m_2} + \frac{\mu_2 m_1}{m_2} + \mu_2\right]$$
$$= g \cos \alpha\left[-\mu_1\left(1 + \frac{m_1}{m_2}\right) + \mu_2\left(1 + \frac{m_1}{m_2}\right)\right]$$
$$= g \cos \alpha\left(1 + \frac{m_1}{m_2}\right)(\mu_2 - \mu_1)$$

Question 23

Given the assumptions detailed in the question, conservation of energy gives the following equation:

Energy required = gravitational potential energy + kinetic energy + work done against air resistance

The gravitational potential energy is the energy required to raise the plane to the height of 11 km:

$$GPE = mgh$$
$$= 3000 \times 10 \times 11 \times 10^3$$
$$330 \times 10^6 \text{ J}$$

The kinetic energy is the energy required to accelerate the plane to its speed of 900 km/h (= 250 ms^{-1}):

$$KE = \frac{1}{2}mv^2$$
$$= \frac{1}{2} \times 3000 \times 250^2$$
$$= 93.75 \times 10^6 \text{ J}$$

The work done against air resistance is given by the equation

$$W = F \times d$$
$$= kv^2 \times d$$
$$= 10^{-3} \times 250^2 \times 556 \times 10^3$$
$$= 34.75 \times 10^6 \text{ J}$$

The total energy required is therefore

$$(330 + 93.75 + 34.75) \times 10^6 = \mathbf{458.5 \ MJ}$$

END OF PAPER

Final Advice

Arrive well rested, well fed and well hydrated

The PAT is an intensive test, so make sure you're ready for it. Ensure you get a good night's sleep before the exam (there is little point cramming) and don't miss breakfast. If you're taking water into the exam then make sure you've been to the toilet before so you don't have to leave during the exam. Make sure you're well rested and fed in order to be at your best!

Move on

If you're struggling, move on. Every question has equal weighting and there is no negative marking. In the time it takes to answer on hard question, you could gain three times the marks by answering the easier ones. Be smart to score points – especially in the multiple-choice section where some questions are far easier than others.

Afterword

Remember that the route to a high score is your approach and practice. Don't fall into the trap that *"you can't prepare for the PAT"*– this could not be further from the truth. With knowledge of the test, some useful time-saving techniques and plenty of practice you can dramatically boost your score.

Work hard, never give up and do yourself justice.

Good luck!

Acknowledgements

I would like to express my sincerest thanks to the many people who helped make this book possible, especially the Oxbridge Tutors who shared their expertise in compiling the huge number of questions and answers.

Rohan

About Us

Infinity Books is the publishing division of *Infinity Education*. We currently publish over 85 titles across a range of subject areas – covering specialised admissions tests, examination techniques, personal statement guides, plus everything else you need to improve your chances of getting on to competitive courses such as medicine and law, as well as into universities such as Oxford and Cambridge.

Outside of publishing we also operate a highly successful tuition division, called UniAdmissions. This company was founded in 2013 by Dr Rohan Agarwal and Dr David Salt, both Cambridge Medical graduates with several years of tutoring experience. Since then, every year, hundreds of applicants and schools work with us on our programmes. Through the programmes we offer, we deliver expert tuition, exclusive course places, online courses, best-selling textbooks and much more.

With a team of over 1,000 Oxbridge tutors and a proven track record, UniAdmissions have quickly become the UK's number one admissions company.

Visit and engage with us at:
Website (Infinity Books): www.infinitybooks.co.uk
Website (UniAdmissions): www.uniadmissions.co.uk
Facebook: www.facebook.com/uniadmissionsuk
Twitter: @infinitybooks7